Praise for *Be a Dime*

"Being aware of your energy and how it impacts others—and yourself—is a skill that Jill Payne's practical teachings and insights can help you master. Once you possess the cheat code to being a *DIME*, your joyful journey through life awaits."

—MICHAEL BARTLETT, President and CEO, Canada Basketball

"With research-backed insights and playful stories, Jill Payne provides readers with the tools they need to shape their daily experience, not only for maximum capacity but for a life brimming with 10-out-of-10 joy. Highly recommended."

—DAN PONTEFRACT, award-winning author of *Work-Life Bloom* and *Lead. Care. Win.*

"*Be a Dime* is indeed a Big Freakin' Deal, and then some. Jill's radiant guide empowers you to rediscover your inner strength and unlock boundless energy. In a world full of challenges, Jill's wisdom inspires us to rise above and aim for a life that's consistently close to a perfect 10."

—ANDREW FERENCE, former NHLer, Stanley Cup champion

BE A DIME

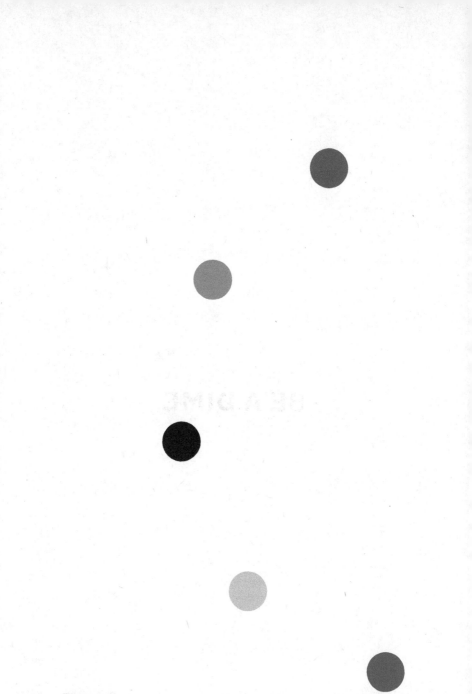

Figure.1
Vancouver / Toronto / Berkeley

JILL PAYNE

BE A DIME

UNLEASH YOUR
INHERENT ENERGY
AND LIVE LIFE
MORE JOYFULLY

Cataloging data is available from Library and Archives Canada
ISBN 978-1-77327-214-6 (pbk.)
ISBN 978-1-77327-215-3 (ebook)
ISBN 978-1-77327-216-0 (pdf)

Cover design by Teresa Bubela
Interior design by Jazmin Welch

Editing by Steve Cameron
Copy editing by Lesley Cameron
Proofreading by Nancy Foran
Indexing by Stephen Ullstrom

Printed and bound in Canada by Friesens

Figure 1 Publishing Inc.
Vancouver BC Canada
www.figure1publishing.com

Figure 1 Publishing works in the traditional, unceded territory of the xʷməθkʷəy̓əm
(Musqueam), Sḵwx̱wú7mesh (Squamish), and səlilwətaɫ (Tsleil-Waututh) peoples.

For Loë

Table of Contents

Introduction

ARE YOU STRUGGLING to find the energy you need to get through your day? Your week? Maybe you don't even have the energy to commit to work deadlines or social commitments. Are you suffering from ennui? Fear? Worry? Anxiety? All of the above?

If you are, you're not alone. And I'm glad you're here.

Let me tell you first off that there is nothing wrong with you. Collectively, we are unhappier than ever. According to Gallup, which began tracking global "well-being," a word the polling organization uses interchangeably with "happiness," global unhappiness has been climbing steadily for over a decade. It's a trend that began well before the COVID-19 pandemic.

Between 2006 and 2022, Gallup conducted more than 5 million interviews, representing more than 98 percent of the world's population. The findings from the study, discussed in a blog post on Gallup's website titled "The Global Rise of Unhappiness," revealed that "people feel more anger, sadness, pain, worry and stress than ever before."[1]

You probably don't need statistics to tell you that. We are living through difficult and divisive times, and you can see, hear, and feel it in the world around you. It can be a daily struggle, and almost impossible, not to let the news and the enormity of the crises facing the world weigh you down. Add your own personal challenges to that societal tension and finding happiness can seem like an insurmountable task.

I want to help fix that. I believe we all have unknown reserves of strength within us, and I want to help you harness energy and vitality so you can live a truly joyful and fulfilled life. All you need is already within you. You just have to learn how to access it.

What is this mysterious "it"? It's your energy, and energy is the magic that changes everything.

In the context of this book and my Be a Dime program, energy is equivalent to capacity, specifically, the capacity to get things done. Simply, when you have more energy, you are bright and focused, your to-do list is easier to accomplish, and you are better prepared to deal with the unexpected.

Energy, in this sense, is not the cellular kind resulting from your metabolism—although a good diet certainly helps—but a system of internal, mental dialogue that, once learned and mastered, will have you brimming with the capacity to rise to meet your daily challenges and live the life you've always wanted.

People who have more capacity to deal with life's ups and downs are following a set of simple steps, either knowingly or unknowingly, and by doing so, are *Diming*.

What is Diming? It's living a life that is consistently as close to 10 out of 10 as possible. Now, before I go any further, let me acknowledge that you can't always be living at a 10. It's unattainable and I know this firsthand. When I created my program and honed my philosophies, I was young and free, had no dependents, and was living on a beach in Costa Rica and running a physical fitness program (one that happened to bring me a few celebrity clients) to make ends meet. The days were long and sun-drenched. My biggest stressor was deciding what time I wanted to go surfing, and sometimes the waves were too loud for me to sleep. I was Diming *hard*.

A decade later, as I'm putting the finishing touches to this book, I'm a single mother who, because of geography, has very little familial support and runs her own coaching and consulting business. While my life is certainly privileged, it is still far more challenging than it was during those blissful Costa Rican days. And let me tell you, despite my best efforts, I'm not a 10 every day. And that's important to keep in mind. A daily Dime isn't realistic, but striving for that goal, and genuinely acknowledging and learning to work through the difficult times while consistently positioning yourself to come back to Dime levels, is energy management at its peak. It's not easy, but it's worth it.

So, how would you describe someone who has energy? Someone who is living as a Dime?

Someone in this state is capacious. They have the ability to adapt to their surroundings; they light up a room; it feels good to be around them; they smile; they get things done; they believe in themselves, trust themselves, and therefore trust the world more. They expect good things to happen. They have an eagerness and excitement for the moment. They speak nicely to themselves. They are focused on things that make them feel good. Their nervous system is calm and alert.

These days we have access to so much information that life can feel overwhelming. Intellectually, we know what we should be doing, but we can't quite figure out how to do it properly. That's not a planning problem, it's a capacity problem. If people had enough capacity to maintain healthy habits, they'd already be maintaining them. People often think that the stars need to align for them—things need to go right—before they can feel good. But the truth is, if you feel good, what's happening around you won't matter quite as much. Having energy simply feels good, and it's within our power to harness that energy on our very own.

That's the promise of this book.

I work with many clients who are physically and mentally tired. It's understandable, given the state and pace of the world. Their brains are constantly running on what needs to happen next, and their lives aren't what they wanted or hoped for. There's fear and uncertainty all around, and that's their focus. While it's hard to ignore current events, and it's human to feel the gravity of them, a cycle of negative thinking is inhibiting us from living a life full of energy.

When energy is poorly managed, people often stifle their ability to think creatively; finding solutions to problems becomes difficult. People in this state feel drained or angry or resentful or resigned. They're in jobs they hate or relationships that aren't working. Or both. They distract themselves with unhealthy food or drugs or alcohol or social media. If they have the desire to change, their first response is to try to force themselves to sleep more, exercise every day, eat perfectly, meditate, take cold showers, and stretch more.

I love all these things and know they will increase your energy, but someone who is not managing their energy from within will not be able to follow through with their well-meaning plans—and they will then feel even worse for letting themselves down.

What the world needs at this moment is to learn how to feel good again. There will always be something to worry about or change or fix outside of us. You can spend your life trying to control all of it, or you can understand that you only have control over yourself and that control starts with the thoughts and feelings that bang around between your ears. In that space between your ears you have the power to create your own experience and work toward being just about anything you desire.

• • •

In the fall of 2019, I was living my dream with the love of my life in New York City. I had an apartment in the financial district and was running a thriving business, traveling from coast to coast on speaking engagements, taking calls from clients when I wasn't taking yoga or spin classes, and having regular lunch dates at the healthiest restaurants in town with my close circle of friends. I picture myself walking through Chinatown, immersed in a juicy podcast, with tons of capacity to create content, think creatively, and stride confidently into my future. It was peak *Sex and the City* and a world away from the small Nova Scotia town I grew up in.

Little did I know everything was about to change.

While I had previously always been in relationships with men, my partner at this time was a woman from Paris who was living in the U.S. while navigating a separation. She swept me off my feet and blindsided me with feelings I had never experienced before. I was all in. The relationship wasn't always easy, but it was deep and passionate, and I saw our future with great clarity.

Part of that future included my desire to become a mother. My partner felt the same way. We were committed to bringing a child into this world. We choose a donor—and boom—two weeks later I was pregnant, after only one try.

And then she left.

I was single, pregnant, and in survival mode. Instead of slowing down to fully process the trauma of my partner's abrupt departure, I kept traveling and speaking. In December 2019, I moved to Victoria, British Columbia, a place I'd lived 10 years prior and where my sister and many friends called home. Three months later, I was standing on stage in Winnipeg, Manitoba, five months pregnant, when the news hit that because of the coronavirus outbreak, everything was shutting down for two weeks. Two weeks! I couldn't imagine sitting still for that long, but suddenly I was loading up on canned goods and gas and searching fruitlessly for toilet paper.

Like most of you, I was rocked to the core by the global pandemic. It made me realize that my Dime lifestyle wasn't feasible or sustainable. The bedrock of my career, of my teaching, was built upon the practice of being a Dime. The pandemic made me see that life has its own ebbs and flows, and sometimes the best you can do is show up with a forced smile on your face.

I had to rethink how my beliefs and lifestyle fit into a whole new paradigm. I simultaneously needed to adapt my teachings to fit into a world that was suffering while using my own strategies more than ever to get back to living a life I recognized and loved. I undertook this work not just for me and the child who was coming into a world full of upheaval, but also for the greater good of the world around me. This was my new para-Dime.

The philosophy underpinning Be a Dime was actually strengthened when stress-tested, but the way I lived and taught it changed. I couldn't spend extended time getting myself to a 10 before leaving the house, and I was living with a lot more uncertainty and anxiety, which made it harder to access the very tools I needed more than ever. Through this I learned how to use these tools more efficiently and effectively and how to weave them into a busier, more stressful life. I also learned to approach clients with more empathy, understanding, and compassion. I became even more passionate about my beliefs after they helped pull me through this dark period of my life and as I prepared to be the best mother I could.

My daughter, my Baby Dime, was born in June 2020. Now I'm bringing this book, which I dedicate to her, into the world. She inspired me to write it, and I hope it will teach her how to live a full, healthy, joyous life.

The pandemic also sharpened my focus on my own privilege bestowed by DNA and geography. Black Lives Matter opened eyes globally to the barriers and injustices faced by marginalized and racialized communities. Canada has been forced to acknowledge its subjugation and genocide of Indigenous communities after finding graves at residential schools. War ravages many countries, climate change continues to wreak havoc on Earth, and intolerance and division are growing. Collectively, we are in anguish.

I now teach my energy management program with a revived sense of compassion and even greater commitment. I know the most helpful thing I can do is share the real goods—the raw truth of what I've experienced and how I apply it to my own life. I created the core tenets of this program 10 years ago, and, through iteration and perspective, I can see the program I deliver now was created for myself. They say the best business plans solve a personal problem. I lacked positivity and natural energy. I needed tools to shift my mood and to be a positive force in the world. I wholeheartedly believe in the strategies I have come up with, and I speak with such passion about them because they've pulled me out of some very low moments. It's not an exaggeration to say they've saved me.

As I neared completion of this book, I was conducting a corporate seminar on energy management. At the end of it, I was hit with some tough questions. I relish the opportunity to challenge my own beliefs and methods, and this was one of those times that gave me pause. There was a discussion around toxic positivity and privilege, and after considering some of the language I use, I think it's important to note that energy management isn't just assessing for positivity.

We are assessing for self-compassion, self-awareness, and self-regulation and the capacity we have within us to access those abilities. When my daughter is banging on pots and pans in her pretend kitchen and I have capacity, I make up songs and sing along. When I don't have capacity and am unable to regulate myself, I may react in a tone that I am not proud of. The situation—the clattering of pots and pans—is the same, but my level of capacity shifts my ability to regulate myself. I won't always have the capacity to make up songs, but if I can have awareness of my capacity in the moment, I may choose to take some deep breaths or speak to myself kindly instead of losing my patience and acting in a way I'd rather not.

Self-compassion and forgiveness are skills most of us don't practice enough, but they're assets that will improve your quality of life in so many ways, including your ability to handle what comes at you. And, as life has taught us, we never know what lies ahead.

My program is not about ignoring your negative emotions and experiences and simply faking or projecting happiness. It's about using the scale of 1 to 10 to become aware of how you are actually feeling and then using the tools within you to regulate yourself. There is power and freedom in knowing you don't need everything to change outside of yourself.

And when you learn to trust your ability to regulate yourself, your nervous system will show up at its best—even when challenged. It takes practice, which means having compassion for yourself during the learning process, but when we can be more self-aware and choose our reactions, we will have energy and capacity to live a life we enjoy and are proud of. We're not ignoring our true and often difficult emotions, we're embracing them and working with them. That is being a Dime.

Every life is unique, but the human condition is universal. Vulnerability is one aspect of the human condition that allows us to connect, and I love feeling connected. I share my story as an example of how I've used the tools outlined in the following pages. You may relate to some of the situations; you'll definitely understand the emotions.

I won't pretend my program will right all the wrongs in the world or lead to a more just society, but if I can bring some peace to an individual struggling with global events or their daily life, I'll consider it a success. The world needs more light, and the rays I'm shining in these pages are my small contribution.

I will set the table for you. I will show you there are new ways of thinking and showing up in the world to bring the most joyful shift in your daily life. You might not be able to change your circumstances, and you certainly can't control the rest of the world, but managing your thoughts and energy is an achievable goal. You have the agency and the ingredients within. I'll help you to choose energy consciously and to make it a habit. If you can manage your energy, you can manage your mental state. That's far more important than what you look like or what you wear or any other external factor you bring to your world.

And remember, tiny steps add up to a great journey. You don't need to know or see the ultimate destination. Just start walking. I recently read an Instagram post by Brianna Wiest, the author of *The Mountain Is You: Transforming Self-Sabotage into Self-Mastery* and *101 Essays That Will Change the Way You Think,* that resonated with me. She wrote:

Every hour is a new beginning—you just don't realize it until you remember that every soul-shifting, life-changing experience you have happens in an otherwise ordinary day. In an instant, you meet a moment that changes your world forever. You find the job, you book the flight, you sign the papers, you choose to make the change that changes it all. Chapters of great transformation often feel like they carry on forever, but the truth is that they are often gardens that grow from tiny seeds that you've been planting for a very long time.

This book is the first step. You are about to turn the page and begin a lifestyle transformation. You will learn how to work toward Diming. Every. Single. Day. I hope reading this plants a tiny seed of positive that grows within you from this day forward.

You're ready to live the life you've always wanted. I want that for you. You want that for you. Let's make it happen!

CHAPTER ONE

An Introduction
to Diming

ON A SCALE of 1 to 10, how do you feel today? How do you feel these days? Really think about it. Consider all areas of your life.

You can imagine that the bottom of that scale is a pretty miserable place to be. It's full of fatigue, sadness, frustration, a lack of motivation, and all of the things that we generally wish to avoid.

The top of the scale is the absolute peak of being. When you're there, you're full of energy, spontaneity, love, passion, drive, and productivity.

So where do you honestly land? My guess (and my hope) is that you aren't all the way down at 1, but I have a feeling you have a way to go to reach 10.

Believe me when I say you can get to 10. It's in you. I know it is.

Yes, emotions can seem elusive and hard to control. For many of us, we wait for conditions to change for us so we can feel a certain way. This is like putting the cart before the horse. Why rely on external stimuli to dictate your mood? That's giving a lot of power to an unpredictable world. Instead, why not take a few simple and effective steps to heighten your energy so that you can be in control of your mood? Our energy determines our mood, and our mood determines our experience of life. When you manage your energy, you manage your emotions, and subsequently your experience of life.

. . . .

Our energy determines our mood, and our mood determines our experience of life.

. . . .

Don't wait for external conditions to change! Be your own advocate, improve your mental state, and watch the conditions follow suit. This is how you climb the scale and learn to live closer to beauty than misery.

This is how you Dime.

Detailed Positive vs. Detailed Negative

I like to think of each of the numbers on the Dime scale of 1 to 10 as a channel. Every day, we tune into different channels at various times. You could start off your day at a 7, move down to a 3 at noon, flip back up to a 5 mid-afternoon, and end your day at an 8. What I want for you is less channel surfing. The goal is for you to use the methods outlined in this book to use your energy management to be able to ride the waves of your day or week and stay consistently where you are, because your channel will directly correlate with what you put out into the world as well as how you receive it.

It goes without saying that you want to be above 5, the center point on your scale, at all times if possible. And the higher, the better!

Consider 5 neutral, neither positive nor negative, and that hovering around this mushy middle is generally negative to generally positive. Above this is what we call being detailed positive. Here there's only opportunity. Detailed positive is a place where the small waves you are riding don't even phase you. Missed the bus? There will be another. Dropped your coffee? It sucks, for sure, but it's also an opportunity to maybe try that new coffee spot you've been eyeing. Similarly, the larger waves are easier to negotiate when you're in a detailed positive frame of mind. Turned down for the promotion you were aiming for? Take some time to let the disappointment sink in and then, *bam!* Your mind brings you back to positive. Perhaps not getting the promotion is a sign that you need to head elsewhere, that you need to think carefully about whether you really wanted it in the first place, or that you need to acknowledge (in a positive way) that you need to work harder to achieve your goals.

Below the line, in a detailed negative space, you are going to find challenges. From a low energy channel, detailed negative feels normal, yet being this way brings us down further. Missed the bus? In detailed negative, while you intellectually know there will be another bus, you'll likely ruminate about how bad transit frequency is, and the negativity that you've let dominate your thoughts might stop you from brainstorming a great idea for a work problem you've been trying to solve.

In detailed negative, the larger waves are much harder to negotiate, and often they can turn you into a self-defeatist. Turned down for the promotion you were aiming for? In detailed negative, not only do you have to let the disappointment sink in, but you'll likely also find yourself deficient in some way, which lowers your channel too. Or you'll jump to victimhood, which is another way we love to stop ourselves from confronting the truth. Maybe you didn't get the promotion because you need to upgrade your skills in some way. If you are detailed negative and practicing victimhood, you'll likely look outward to blame someone else instead of looking inward and seizing the opportunity to grow.

* * * * * * * * * * * *

It's human nature to dwell on the negative, but we give it more power by feeding it.

* * * * * * * * * * *

It's human nature to dwell on the negative, but we give it more power by feeding it, and the details are the fuel. Dwelling on the negative is also catching. People often connect through sharing detailed negative experiences.

One of the best examples I have of this comes from when I was traveling on a speaking tour with the CEO and a human resources specialist from a large corporation. I love HR people. They always crave connection and often value it over all else, and I was particularly fond of this one. She'd heard me speak on several occasions, so she should have been aware of what she did when we arrived at one of the branch offices, a little late and a lot frazzled after a long day of travel.

She worked at head office in a different city and was excited to meet her HR colleagues in person for the first time, but upon entering a conference room full of them, she proceeded to detail all the ways her travel day had gone wrong, gaining negative momentum as she went.

What do you think the other HR people in the room did? Without missing a beat, they immediately started commiserating! They shared stories, at length, of terrible travel experiences they'd had. I sat there, observing this encounter, and thought, "This is exactly why we need to talk about the snowball of negativity rolling downhill and examine it."

It's a trend that many of us are familiar with—jumping on the negativity bandwagon. Instead of having a positive and uplifting connection, like they all wanted, everyone in the room ultimately ended up leaving the conversation riled up after reliving these less-than-ideal experiences.

But it was great material for my talk later.

You may be asking yourself, "What's so bad about bonding over something as typical as a bad travel day? Those HR people likely enjoyed sharing similar experiences and were able to connect with one another in a genuine way. Isn't that good?"

The problem is that your nervous system (and there's plenty on the nervous system to come) gets activated when you tell these stories, and without a sense of time, it relives the same feelings you had in the moment. So, in the HR travel example, I'm suddenly faced by a roomful of people in a state of stress and agitation, feeding off each other as the negativity beast grows and takes over the space. It's contagious, and it will drop everyone down the Dime scale.

It is human nature to dwell on the negative, so it's up to us to use the tools we have to combat this instinct and focus on the positives. Remember, just as our negativity has the power to bring down everyone around us, our positivity has the power to lift them up. And while it can make you feel like an empath and a good listener to encourage someone to vent and share details, the truly loving response is to steer the conversation in a positive direction for them.

When I first started teaching this material, I would have said that if someone is negative, just stay away from them, they aren't on your channel. However, I've learned that that is not a kind response. We all experience moments on low channels. We have to honor that. We are living through a human experience that gives us a wildly disparate range of emotions. One day you may be the person on the low channel, and you won't want to be ignored or dismissed because of it.

10 – DETAILED POSITIVE (DIME STATE)

9

8   Above the line =

7   Opportunity

6

5 – NEUTRAL (HOPEFUL STATE)

4

3   Below the line =

              Problems

2

1 – DETAILED NEGATIVE (SUFFERING STATE)

If someone is living in a detailed negative space, they want to feel heard and to have their feelings validated. Sometimes the reason they continue to go into detail is that they feel the person they are speaking to isn't listening or doesn't get it. When we try with the best of intentions to get someone to talk about something positive, we can come across as not listening, which makes them talk more about the negatives.

What we need to do is catch them before they get to detailed negative, when they're at generally negative, and at that point in the conversation, when it is trending upward, compassionately say things like "Wow, I hear you and I imagine you feel this way."

Then you can say things like "What could you do for the rest of the afternoon that would make you feel better?" Or, "What is the ideal situation?" Or, "I love you too much to let you go there. I know you will feel worse and so will I."

A compassionate sentence will be well received. We can also speak to ourselves that way when we notice that we are getting negative internally. I notice my own micro moments of resistance to life and how it creates tension in my body. When I first become aware that I'm trending to a negative space, I consciously decide to pull myself out of it by shifting my focus and asking myself a question that can cut across the negativity and get my mind thinking of the detailed positive that can result from my detailed negative thinking.

Trevor Moawad, who was the performance coach of the Denver Broncos quarterback Russell Wilson, likened this inner dialogue to the concept of getting to neutral.[1] The idea is that moving from a deeply negative place to a positive place is often too much of a leap and so feels inauthentic. Moving all the way from detailed negative to detailed positive in one step would risk veering into toxic positivity— pretending everything is fine when it truly isn't. When bad things happened on the football field, Moawad would have his team focus on *not* vocalizing negative thoughts. It may seem like a simple action, but it is powerful in practice, especially in a group setting. Next time you're with a group of people and you're tempted to voice a negative thought, don't, and see where that action takes you and your group.

Being detailed positive, especially in the face of adversity, might feel like an insurmountable task for you. And if this is the way you feel, you aren't alone. According to a study in *Psychological Bulletin*, "There is ample empirical evidence for an asymmetry in the way that adults use positive versus negative information to make sense of their world; specifically, across an array of psychological situations and tasks, adults display a negativity bias, or the propensity to attend to, learn from, and use negative information far more than positive information."[2]

In other words, the proverbial cards are stacked against you. I never said that Diming was going to be easy, only that the rewards of a life full of energy and vitality are well worth the effort.

So, what can you do to shift from negative to neutral and from neutral to positive? I'm glad you asked, as that's the whole point of this book!

How Our Internal Energy Impacts Our External Reality (and Vice Versa)

• •

Tam Hunt trained in evolutionary biology before becoming an environmental lawyer focused on renewable energy law and policy. He is the co-developer, with Professor Jonathan Schoole, of the general resonance theory of consciousness and has published a number of peer-reviewed articles on the study of consciousness. His studies show that:

> All things in our universe are constantly in motion, vibrating. Even objects that appear to be stationary are in fact vibrating, oscillating, resonating, at various frequencies. Resonance is a type of motion, characterized by oscillation between two states. And ultimately all matter is just vibrations of various underlying fields. An interesting phenomenon occurs when different vibrating things/processes come into proximity: they will often start, after a little time, to vibrate together at the same frequency. They "sync up," sometimes in ways that can seem mysterious. This is described today as the phenomenon of spontaneous self-organization.

Essentially, Hunt believes that "it is all about vibrations, but it's also about the type of vibrations and, most importantly, about shared vibrations."[3]

In other words, your vibrational state can impact those around you. And when you start to live at a higher level on the Dime scale, you have the power to subconsciously alter the people around you with your own positive vibrations. On the flipside, unfiltered external vibrations can have a negative effect on us, which reinforces the importance of recognizing how outside factors play a role in our energy and how we can face and mitigate them.

In an article titled "Effects of Internal and External Environment on Health and Well-being: From Cell to Society," Dr. Andrea Tomljenović from the Institute for Anthropological Research in Zagreb, Croatia, explains:

> Every single cell in an organism is influenced by its microenvironment and surrounding cells. Biology, psychology, emotions, spirit, energy, lifestyle, culture, economic and political influences, social interactions in family, work, living area, and the possibilities to expresses oneself and live a full life with a sense of well-being have influence on people's appearances. Disease is as much social as biological. It is a reaction of an organism to unbalancing changes in the internal environment caused by the changes in the external environment and/or by the structural and functional failures or unfortunate legacies. Health gradient in the society depends on the everyday circumstances in which people live and work. The health of the population is an insight into the society.[4]

The suggestion here is that the micro leads to the macro and vice versa. The tiniest pieces of us—our cells—

can ultimately change society, as healthy members of society create a healthy environment for all, and a healthy environment has a major impact on the wellness (and energy) of those who live in it. They reflect each other, and Tomljenović's argument is that more psychology and anthropology should be introduced into the study of physical health and medicine. You can take this holistic approach with yourself: improve your internal energy to create a more positive external environment, and allow a healthy external world to be reflected internally.

Some of our individual problems can be a reflection of the physical energy channel we're on. If you're on a low channel, challenges will find you. You will perceive situations as obstacles rather than stepping stones. If you have low energy, you will draw negativity.

If you're positive, you're going to experience the world and the people around you warmly. You're going to see the good in scenarios in ways you hadn't before and receive the positivity you put out. Positivity can become a self-fulfilling prophecy.

Challenges can be a blessing. Franklin D. Roosevelt is credited with saying that "a smooth sea never made a skilled sailor." Storms will come, and they will teach you to be a more resilient person and more skilled at facing turmoil.

To extend the maritime metaphor, when I was a sprint canoeist, I discovered that strong headwinds make us work harder and become stronger.

An example of the upside of strong headwinds from the extreme end of the scale is the philosophy of Viktor Frankl, a Holocaust survivor, psychiatrist, and psychotherapist who developed the school of psychotherapy called logotherapy. It's also known as the third Viennese school of psychotherapy, after the first school (Sigmund Freud's) and the second (Alfred Adler's). Frankl's theory is that the primary motivation of an individual is the search for meaning in life, and the aim of psychotherapy should be to help the individual find that meaning.

In his book *Man's Search for Meaning*, Frankl tells the story of how he survived Auschwitz by finding personal meaning in the experience, which gave him the will to live. His core belief is that a person's main motivation in life is a "will to meaning," even in the most difficult of circumstances. "What man actually needs is not a tensionless state but rather the striving and struggling for a worthwhile goal, a freely chosen task. What he needs is not the discharge of tension at any cost, but the call of a potential meaning waiting to be fulfilled by him."[5]

The way you face your day is a reflection of the channel you're on, and you can learn to change that channel, which is incredibly empowering. If you've been feeling low for a long time and you realize you've been blaming this thing or that person, it's liberating to acknowledge that you can take the wheel and steer your ship.

"Actually, I decide!"

• • •

To be clear, though, you can't just make yourself happy. You can, however, start moving incrementally from detailed negative to generally negative to neutral to generally positive to detailed positive. And with every step toward 10 on the Dime scale, you will be increasing your energy. Higher energy will result in a better, more positive outlook on life and a happier emotional state. Moving along this scale is a self-fulfilling prophecy, and to help you harness all the power within you to help you on your journey, I will share three core principles with you in this book that will enable you to control your channel, manage your energy, and live the life you deserve. I call them B.F.D.

The best part of B.F.D. is that it's always within your power. What you do with your body, what you choose to focus on, and what you decide to say to yourself will always be your choice. When I was going through a breakup and then a pandemic, and when I was raising a child alone, I still had agency, even if I lost sight of that sometimes.

B.F.D. is practical and doable. I know, because I've done it and I've coached countless others who are now Diming. I have felt the energy shift in myself and seen it shift in others, and unlike a physical transformation that can take weeks to notice, this change in thought patterns can be immediate.

B.F.D. is the foundation of Be a Dime. We'll explore each component of it in the coming chapters.

Yes, it's a Big Freakin' Deal, and yes, you can Be a Freakin' Dime. But B.F.D. actually stands for:

BODY.

FOCUS.

DIALOGUE.

CHAPTER TWO

Body

LET'S TALK ABOUT the body. It's a wonder of evolution. It's also the easiest access point to our energy and the first place we can start to manage it. What do I mean by "manage it"?

We hold our psychology in our physiology. Or put another way, the way we carry ourselves—the choices we make in regards to how we move our bodies—can directly impact the way we think and feel.

I admit that it can sound a little hippy-dippy to hear someone tell you that all you need to do to be happy is to smile. But guess what? It's true![1]

Our physiology has such a tremendous and near-immediate impact on our psychology that it is astonishing to me how many people are unaware of the feel-good resource they literally have at their fingertips. (Try the author Mel Robbins's high-five habit, where you literally high-five your reflection. Tell me *that* doesn't boost your happiness.)

Emotions don't just live in the mind. The body carries so much of them as well. A 2010 study separated two strangers by a barrier and asked one of them to touch the other's forearm. The person doing the touching had a list of emotions that they had to communicate simply by touching the other person's forearm for one second per emotion. The person who was being touched had to guess which emotion was being conveyed. The results were astonishing.

"Given the number of emotions being considered, the odds of guessing the right emotion by chance were about eight percent," wrote Dacher Keltner, one of the researchers involved in the study. "But remarkably, participants guessed compassion correctly nearly 60 percent of the time. Gratitude, anger, love, fear—they got those right more than 50 percent of the time as well."[2]

We still lag behind our primate cousins in conveying feeling and connectedness through touch, and North American *Homo sapiens* are generally pretty far behind the rest of the world when it comes to physical contact, though.

In the 1960s, the psychologist Sidney Jourard conducted a study by observing friends having conversations in cafés. The results showed that in England, on average, the friends did not touch each other at all over the course of an hour. In the United States, they touched twice an hour on average. But in France, the average number of touches was 110 per hour, and that shot up to 180 in Puerto Rico!

More recently, the Johns Hopkins neuroscientist David J. Linden proved the power of touch in his 2015 book *Touch: The Science of Hand, Heart, and Mind*. He writes that it's the first sense to develop in the womb and that our skin is a "social organ" that improves health and enhances development. He cites research that hugging among professional basketball players improves team performance and that premature babies are more likely to survive if they're regularly held by their parents instead of being kept in incubators. Children deprived of touch also grow up with more developmental difficulties.[3]

Considering the importance of touch, it's no surprise that with social distancing and the slow return to comfortable physical contact, depression and loneliness have skyrocketed since the pandemic began.

Granted, we have a lot more awareness of consent now than people did when Jourard conducted his study, but among friends we still don't express ourselves physically nearly as much as we should. A simple touch on the arm can convey warmth, sympathy, appreciation, joy, or understanding. Imagine what a hug can do!

Moving up the scale toward being a Dime starts with getting in touch with our own body. When we make the effort to move our bodies in certain simple ways, we are telling our nervous system to see the world differently. We're telling it that we're ready to take on any challenge and that we're not living in fear or shame.

In my corporate work, I have one client who manages a diverse team of people in a customer-facing position as a franchisee. It can be a hard and thankless job some days, and this client wore the difficulty of her day in how she physically presented herself. In our work together I've encouraged her to walk with a strong posture, smiling, breathing deeply, and swinging her arms energetically. I've also managed to improve her presence by getting her to speak clearly and confidently. The result? Her staff have taken notice, and her positive energy is rubbing off on them. As her staff mirror her, the change becomes self-sustainable and trickles down all the way to the clients they interact with. A higher energy from the top pervades the workplace and creates a more positive and successful franchise.

When your physical presence changes, you will get a positive reaction from the people around you—all because you chose to physically manifest the thoughts and feelings you wanted to project out into the world. But that's not the goal, that's a bonus. The goal is that you, yourself, will feel calmer, more joyful, and more capable.

There are five ways we can all shift our bodies and create energy. They can be quick and subtle, or they can be more deliberate, and if you stick with them through any awkward first efforts, soon they'll become habit. They aren't cure-alls for what you might be facing in your life, but they're a tremendous start and part of your toolkit for facing the world when you feel like you're falling below the line and stress is starting to get the better of you. They are:

- Posture
- Smiling
- Breathing
- Voice
- Movement

Posture

The social psychologist Amy Cuddy gave a TED Talk on power posing that's garnered over 68.5 million views, making it one of the most popular in the history of the series.[4] I highly recommend it.

After suffering a traumatic brain injury in a car accident as a young woman, Cuddy wasn't expected to regain full mental capacity, but she's now a professor and researcher at Harvard Business School. She studies how nonverbal behavior, including body position, can influence other people and your own brain.

Cuddy suggests that standing in a posture of confidence, even when you aren't feeling confident, can create that feeling and have a positive impact on your chances for success. Our body language governs how we think and feel about ourselves and, thus, how we hold our bodies can have an impact on our minds. By commanding a powerful stance, we can actually make ourselves feel more powerful.

"Let your body tell you you're powerful and deserving, and you become more present, enthusiastic and authentically yourself," Cuddy is quoted as saying.[5]

Cuddy supported her power posing hypothesis through a study that she conducted among Columbia University students. Participants sat in either a high-power pose (an expansive posture) or a low-power pose (leaning inward, legs crossed) for two minutes. The research team found that those who sat in the high-power pose felt more powerful and performed better in mock interviews than those who sat in the low-power pose.[6]

In an article in the *New York Times*, Cuddy is quoted as explaining that "lab participants who spent two minutes in a room alone doing high-power poses (feet on the desk with fingers laced behind the head, let's say) increased testosterone levels by about 20 percent and lowered the stress hormone cortisol by about 25 percent."[7]

So, check in with your posture, or audit your body, as Cuddy suggests. Is your chest lifted? Are your shoulders down? Are you feeling tall through the spine? Are you pushing down through your sit bones (also known as sitz bones, they're at the bottom of your pelvis and what you're balancing on when you're sitting up straight) and reaching the crown of your head to the sky? If you are below 5 on the Dime scale, I'm going to assume that your posture probably isn't great. Maybe your shoulders are slumped, or you routinely cast your gaze downward. This state of being doesn't project confidence, and that's reflected internally. But you can begin to alter your state by making the smallest of changes. A woman I know who was living with depression received a valuable suggestion from her therapist. He suggested that when she walked to work, she should look at the rooftops. She noticed when she started to do this that her chest was lifted, her head was up, her shoulders were back, her diaphragm was expanded, and she was breathing better. It was simple but powerful, and it changed the way she started every day.

Another way to change your posture and energy is to close your eyes and imagine how you'd hold your body if you were a 10 on the Dime scale right now. Try a quick power pose while you're reading. Stand up, put your hands on your hips, lift your chest, and put a nice smile on your face. Once you're finished, check in on your posture again. I like to ask my audiences to do this as a group. You would be amazed by how alive the space feels once everyone has struck their pose. (Or maybe you wouldn't be amazed because you are actually feeling it yourself right now.)

In my seminars, I've noticed that even saying the word "posture" immediately changes everyone's body position. The reaction is audible to me on the stage and throughout the theater as people adjust themselves.

We all instinctively know what good posture looks and feels like—it is strong, stable, and empowering. However, it's easy to slip back into bad habits, so try to remind yourself to check in on your posture throughout the day. Ask yourself how you would sit, how you would stand, how you would walk, if you were a 10. Repeat this to yourself and pose powerfully as needed.

Amy Cuddy's studies have shown a change in biochemistry in two minutes of power posing, so do three!

Smiling

Show me those teeth!

If I were to take you on as a personal training client now, I might have you adopt a power pose, ask you to smile, and then tell you I'll be back at the end of our session. Or I might have you walk to work looking at the rooftops with a big smile plastered on your face—head up, eyes up, chest up, diaphragm and mouth open. People might wonder who this confident, joyous person is, and you might wonder how you arrived at work with such energy and confidence.

. . . .

"Each time you smile, you throw a little feel-good party in your brain."

. . . .

Smiling with your teeth showing signals happiness, both to yourself and to the world around you. And if a big, wide-open smile seems unnatural, that means you're not doing it nearly enough!

The behavioral psychologist Sarah Stevenson says, "Each time you smile, you throw a little feel-good party in your brain."[8]

Dopamine and serotonin—the brain's feel-good chemical messengers, or neurotransmitters—are activated when you smile. Many people take medication to increase and regulate their levels of these chemicals. The simple act of smiling can lessen symptoms of anxiety and depression.

Endorphins, the body's natural pain relievers and very own opiates, also flood the brain when you smile. It's the same natural high that athletes chase with a good run or workout, but when you don't have time for that, a big smile is a great shortcut to the feeling.

And for those who crave line-free living, facial fillers can trick you into feeling better because they inhibit frowning. A study at the University of Cardiff in Wales looked at how Botox "treatments affect the patients' psychological responses as well as their muscular actions and appearance of lines." The results showed that "there was a decrease in negative mood following treatment for the participants who received the BTX [Botox] treatment for frown lines."[9]

Another study, this one conducted at the University of South Australia, found that when participants were forced to smile by holding a pen between their teeth, they were more likely to interpret stimuli positively. The facial muscles told the brain they were happy. Specifically, the brain's emotional center, the amygdala, was stimulated and released neurotransmitters to unlock a feeling of joy.

The study's chief investigator, Dr. Fernando Marmolejo-Ramos, is quoted as saying, "When your muscles say you're happy, you're more likely to see the world around you in a positive way."[10]

If those two experiments aren't enough to convince you, a team at the University of Tennessee at Knoxville conducted a meta-analysis of 138 similar studies, which included a total of more than 11 thousand participants. They concluded that, yes, smiling makes people happier, scowling makes them angrier, and frowning makes them sadder.

According to Nicholas Coles, the lead researcher on the study, "These findings are exciting because they provide a clue about how the mind and the body interact to shape our conscious experience of emotion. We still have a lot to learn about these facial feedback effects, but this meta-analysis put us a little closer to understanding how emotions work."[11]

A fun and easy way to give yourself a big smile is to imagine you're about to go into a party that's being held in your honor. How exciting is that? Think about the anticipation and happiness that would fill you at that moment.

Or, if parties aren't your thing, think about when you were last truly happy. What moment brought you there? Where were you? What were you feeling? Who were you with?

One surefire way for me to bring on a smile is to reflect on moments with my daughter. We all have something like that we can draw on to tap into our own reservoir of happiness.

Now let those emotions shine from your face! Your smile shows warmth and joy, and it acts as a mirror—the positivity you project is reflected back to you in kind, increasing the feeling exponentially.

As noted in an article in *Royal Society Publishing* called "Evidence for Mirror Systems in Emotions," "Let your inner energy show on the outside and see how that broadcasting bounces off others and back to you."[12]

Laughter Truly Is the Best Medicine

Just ask science! According to the Mayo Clinic, "A good laugh has great short-term effects. When you start to laugh, it doesn't just lighten your load mentally, it actually induces physical changes in your body. . . . [It] isn't just a quick pick-me-up, though. It's also good for you over the long term."

Breathing

Don't be shallow! Your breath is meant to be deep. Fill your lungs and your belly.

In and out.

In and out.

In . . . and . . . out.

Breath lives in our chest when we're in a heightened emotional state and in our belly when we're resting and recovering. These functions are governed by your sympathetic and parasympathetic nervous systems, respectively. When your sympathetic nervous system is activated by stressors, you can hyperventilate, especially when you're in a state of panic and anxiety. You can even trigger this by taking shallow, short breaths.[13]

The fight-or-flight response is a physiological reaction to something that your mind perceives to be stressful or frightening. This perception activates the sympathetic nervous system and triggers an acute stress response, which prepares the body to do battle or to flee. These responses are evolutionary, developed in early humans to help them survive threatening situations, and they still live in the less evolved part of our brains.

Neurons in the brain stem send epinephrine, acetylcholine, and other chemicals like adrenaline into your body. These cause a rapid increase in heart rate and breathing and dilated pupils, which all happens subconsciously and in roughly half a second. People feel stressed because the fight-or-flight response was designed to "recruit almost all of your being—your mind, body, eyes, everything," says the Stanford University neurobiologist Andrew Huberman. "Meaning, it's going to be very hard to prevent the stress response from happening."[14]

The fight-or-flight response has unhealthy effects if it lasts for any extended period. Its original purpose was to protect us from a short-term threat, such as fighting a wild animal or fleeing from it. While we rarely encounter wild animals on the loose these days, our fight-or-flight response can be triggered in different ways—by an overflowing inbox or a shocking grocery bill or being in crowds, especially after months of social distancing and self-isolating.

Even something like phone separation anxiety is a constant stressor the vast majority of us deal with. Think about it. How many times have you felt a phantom vibration in your pocket? How many times in the last hour have you checked to see where your phone is or if you have any notifications? Most phones can tell you how many times per hour they're picked up. If you're brave enough to look, I bet you'll be shocked at just how often you grabbed that gadget. Next time you go to reach for it, take a few deep breaths instead. Trust me, TikTok (for those of you in Gen Z) or that Facebook picture posted by your high school crush (for Gen Xers) can wait.

So when you feel your heart or mind racing, don't give into that experience. Instead, breathe deeply. You'll find center and balance, because the evolved part of our brain can override the primitive part.

According to a study published in the *Journal of Neurophysiology*, controlling your breathing by counting breaths influences "neuronal oscillations throughout the brain," particularly in brain regions related to emotion.[15] What does that mean? Read on just a little further.

Participants in this particular study were asked to count how many breaths they took over a two-minute period, which made them pay close attention to their breathing.

When they counted correctly, their brain activity in regions related to emotion, memory, and awareness showed a more organized pattern than is normally seen during a state of calm.

In layperson's terms, when we take and release deep and intentional breaths, our brain activity is less scattered. And when we are less scattered, we exact influence over our mood and stress levels; we activate our parasympathetic nervous system. This quiets the sympathetic nervous system and reduces stress and anxiety.

"It is not possible to turn the sympathetic nervous system off completely, but I think of shifting one's breathing to a modulated, slow, relaxed pattern of not overly deep inhales and exhales as a way to turn the volume down on it," explains Kristoffer Rhoads, a clinical neuropsychologist at the University of Washington Medicine Memory and Brain Wellness Center.[16]

Conscious, controlled breathing increases blood flow and oxygen and makes us calm, centered, creative, and connected. But it's not just the C's; it's also some P's—we're able to be present and proactive.

Slow and deliberate breathing, especially diaphragmatic breathing into the belly, which is often used in meditation, also helps regulate our nervous system by stimulating the vagus nerve and activating the relaxation response in the parasympathetic system.[17] And when we're not in survival mode, we can look up and around and assess a situation rationally. That's proactivity versus reactivity. It's how we remain calm, and it allows us to enter a state of flow—when we're completely immersed in an activity—and access our creativity. (It's no coincidence that this kind of control is a common trait in the most successful people in both athletics and the corporate world.)

If you feel anxiety or stress rising, or if you want to activate your parasympathetic system and feel more focused and centered, there's a technique you've probably heard of but rarely practiced. It goes like this:

Sit or stand up straight and breathe in through your nose and down to your belly.

Hold your breath for a moment and exhale slowly through your mouth.

Now do it again.

Pause. There's no rush.

One more time.

This time, smile when you exhale.

Remind yourself that solutions are coming. Let it go.

You can also practice breathing into your diaphragm by lying down with a book on your belly. Push it up and down by breathing in and out. We're so used to chest breathing that it takes some time to learn to breathe into the belly and send a message to your nervous system that all is well and you're safe.

Or try Huberman's breathing technique, called physiological sighs. It's a pattern of breathing in which two inhales through the nose are followed by an extended exhale through the mouth. He explains:

You have little sacks of air in the lungs, which increase the volume of air that you can bring in. Those sacks collapse over time, and as a result, oxygen levels start to go down and carbon dioxide levels go up in the bloodstream and body, and that's a big part of the signaling of the stress response.

The double inhale of the physiological sigh "pops" the air sacks (called alveoli) open, allowing oxygen in and enabling you to offload carbon dioxide in the long, exhaled sigh out.[18]

When you focus on your breathing, you'll feel your energy shift, and when your energy shifts, it can move a whole room. Try it the next time you have a meeting or walk into a party and see what happens. You may be surprised by just how powerful you can be.

Self-regulation is the essence of being a Dime, and regulating your breathing and nervous system is integral to lifting your channel. You have it within you to change your energy, to work toward the next rung on the Dime scale. It's an individual power and responsibility, and even a slight change in breathing can elevate your mood and radiate outward, influencing those around you.

Voice

"The voice is like an iceberg, with parts you see and hear above the water line and parts you don't see but you know are there," according to Bonnie Gross, the founder and president of SpeechScience. "The obvious parts offer clues to the speaker's gender, nationality, and general age. The aspects we react to subconsciously include the speaker's confidence level, maturity, sincerity, and intelligence, among other things."[19]

Consider how you sound when you speak. Do you sound fearful? Hopeful? Certain?

If you're feeling like a 10, your voice will be certain. At a 5, your voice will be hopeful. Your fearful voice resides at the bottom of the scale. Certainty in your voice creates a positive reaction not only in those you speak to but within yourself as well.

"Our voices literally speak for us and about us," says Judith Humphrey, founder of The Humphrey Group and author of *Speaking as a Leader and Taking the Stage*. "The tone of our voice tells our audience whether we believe in what we are saying or are just mouthing the words. It tells them whether we are excited, engaged, inspired, or just plain bored. The pace of our voice tells our audience whether we are nervous or not, confident or not . . . It is our voice that brings our ideas to life and brings us to the hearts and minds of our audience."[20]

Humphrey and her colleagues are especially interested in "helping women unlock the power of their voices."

Women have always walked a fine line in the business world, whether it involves clothing or assertiveness or networking. It's a balancing act I've lived and observed. We have been conditioned to minimize ourselves, but it's time to speak up. Our voices have power.

Wherever you fall on the gender spectrum, speaking like a 10 can command attention, spur others to action, and help you achieve your goals.

"Simply put, our vocal imprint contributes much more than we think to our success, both personally and professionally, even contributing to perceived attractiveness and charisma," state the language and communications specialist and trainer at the United Nations Secretariat Dan Bullock and NYU professor in business communication and linguistics Raúl Sánchez in a *Harvard Business Review* article titled "Don't Underestimate the Power of Your Voice."

"Through our voices, we create nuances of meaning, convey our emotions, and find the secret to communicating our executive presence—that elusive quality we value in leaders who seem to naturally exude confidence and influence. Like fingerprints, no two voices have the same characteristics. Every one of us has a unique vocal image."[21]

According to Bullock and Sánchez, we do all of this through "vocalics," which includes volume, intonation, and rhythm. Volume isn't simply turning up the sound. It's the practice of intentionally placing the emphasis on certain words and, in doing so, directing the conversation to where you want it to go. It doesn't have to be dramatic. "Even the slightest nuances can dramatically shift the meaning of your sentences, express your underlying intentions, and impact how your messages are interpreted." To illustrate their point, they give the example of being in a meeting. If you emphasize the word or phrase most important to you, it will guide the discussion in that direction and essentially indicate what you want a response to. Bullock and Sánchez note that "verbs, adjectives, nouns, and adverbs tend to be focus words as they carry the most meaning when we speak" and that "accentuating keywords [creates] what linguists call 'information focus.'"[22]

Your speech style is also dictated by intonation, the rising or falling of your voice to indicate grammatical meaning—whether something is a statement or a question—or attitude, to express joy, sadness, sarcasm, surprise, etc.

If your intonation goes down instead of up at the end of a sentence, you may also sound more confident and declarative. Upspeak, the practice of making statements sound like questions, can make you sound like you're questioning yourself. Filler words and phrases (maybe, I guess, um, you know) and tag questions (Okay? Don't you think?) also convey a powerless speech style, and hesitancy will make listeners question your confidence or credibility. These are the ways we speak when we're below 5.

Rhythm and melody create what's called voiced punctuation, a method for adding compelling pauses and drama. For example, if you pause, you create anticipation, which is then satisfied when you offer the response or answer. A pause can also give people time to digest and consider what you want them to pay attention to. Try this by separating your own sentences into different thought groups—words that belong together, which you'll recognize because they tend to have natural vocal pauses between them—and seeing how they sound when spoken aloud.

In the article, Bullock and Sánchez use upper-casing and underlining to highlight focus words to compare two ways of responding during a salary negotiation:

"I think I'd like to accept the <u>OFFER</u> / but umm I also want to ask for a 15 percent <u>SALARY</u> increase / <u>OKAY</u>?"

"I'll <u>ACCEPT</u> the offer / with a <u>15 percent</u> salary increase."

Thought groups in the first sentence are combined with uncertainty and the wrong focus words, which indicates weakness in an ongoing negotiation. In the second sentence, thought groups, a powerful speaking style, and focus words emphasize the acceptance of final terms of the salary. It's less of a negotiation and more of a statement.

By learning to use all the techniques I've described in this section, you can assert yourself and express your desires with a direct and confident tone in your voice. An above-the-line voice ensures your message is clear, which benefits both you and whoever is listening. A projection of self-belief creates belief in others.

Like the other aspects of energy management within the body, projecting self-belief takes practice. People spend years trying to master the nuances of speech and their own nerves. Try it in front of a mirror, or record yourself and listen carefully when you play the recording back. You'll be able to hear as your voice goes up and down the scale. Focus on the confident statements and how they sound. Can you take it to Dime level? Listen to when you drop below the line. How you can you level that up, both through the content and how you express it?

Confident speakers are rarely born. They're made. And when you stand up straight, smile, and take a few deep belly breaths before speaking, you're already on your way to having a more powerful, persuasive voice.

Movement

As a former personal trainer, I know that people have a love-hate relationship with their bodies. To help move from the latter to the former, many people seek out a trainer to tell them what to do and to give them prescriptive plans. Their goal of achieving better fitness is admirable, but it often manifests itself in overexercising and undereating, both of which are counterproductive and unhealthy, for body and mind. In my experience, only 10 percent of people manage to follow through on pursuing their fitness goals. (The other

90 percent? They're the ones who would hide from me when I saw them in the grocery store!)

What was it about the 10 percent who stuck with it? You guessed it! They were already living closer to a 10 on the Dime scale. Their motivation to follow through came from within. It was a choice they made for themselves, and the more they did it the better they felt. They woke up and wanted to go to the gym or for a hike; they opened the fridge and chose healthy foods. They created a positive snowball effect.

For myself and in my career, however, I realized that if my goal was to help people live their lives to the fullest, I needed to leave personal training. I wanted the best for my clients, but expecting folks who are at a 3 or 4 on the Dime scale to power through without giving them the tools to achieve the transformation they wanted wasn't fair. Their inability to stick to the exercise and diet regime I set for them would create a shame circle. It would become another way in which they felt they had let themselves down, further dropping them down the scale. It would create a negative snowball effect. I was setting them up for failure, and by extension, I was failing too.

My eureka moment came when I realized that the 90 percent of folks who couldn't keep up with personal training and then hid from me at the grocery store weren't suffering from a lack of willpower to commit to the program. Instead, they were suffering from a lack of *energy*.

Let me be the first to tell you that not having the willpower to do something is *not* a character flaw. It simply means you do not have the energy to push yourself to make the changes you desperately desire. Change, by its very nature, is difficult—no matter how small or large. All change takes effort, and all effort requires energy.

So, like all the concepts that underlie the Body component of B.F.D., you can slowly and incrementally add in the movement portion to *improve* your energy. You don't need to commit to an Olympic athlete's training routine. Just move!

"Any amount of activity is better than none at all," according to an article published by the Mayo Clinic titled "Exercise: 7 Benefits of Regular Physical Activity." If you are currently low on the movement scale, going for a walk or taking the stairs instead of the elevator will be enough to kick-start this part of your program. The benefits you'll realize by adding more movement to your life will be both mental and physical.

"Physical activity stimulates various brain chemicals that may leave you feeling happier, more relaxed and less anxious. Exercise delivers oxygen and nutrients to your tissues and helps your cardiovascular system work more efficiently. And when your heart and lung health improve, you have more energy to tackle daily chores."[23]

The Mayo Clinic recommends at least 150 minutes of moderate aerobic activity a week, but it's not so much about how much you move your body, it's more about how you do it. The more *of* your body you move, the more energy you feel. Move more of your body and you'll start to feel powerful.

. . . .

The more *of* your body you move, the more energy you feel.

. . . .

Move with intent! Walk *BIG*. Swing your arms, lift your knees, and feel the energy course through your body. Imagine walking somewhere with purpose, with conviction. Be noticed. You can use your body to create the energy you need to climb the scale. Get yourself above the line and take big strides toward the Dime. (#WalkBig)

The episode of *Friends* called "The One Where Phoebe Runs" has always stayed with me. The premise is that Rachel won't go jogging with Phoebe because she is embarrassed by Phoebe's wide-legged bounding and wild arm-swinging. Phoebe explains that she only liked running when she was a kid and could go wild without caring what people thought.

Phoebe had a point. Jogging isn't always the most enjoyable activity, but children tear around without a trace of self-consciousness or a care in the world. It's unbridled and natural and fun.

Be a Phoebe! Not only will your body thank you for the exercise and endorphin rush, but you'll also feel an unrestrained joy that's rare in adulthood. I promise it'll bring a smile to your face.

When it comes to movement, most people cite time as their biggest constraint to being more active. If only they had *more* time, they say. But you don't need to commit to going to the gym three times a week or be a part of a regularly scheduled league with teammates relying on you to add movement to your day. All you need is your body and a plan.

I find the easiest, least time-draining way to add to your daily movement is to create a morning routine. What you do in the first hour of your morning can also determine the course of your whole day.

Start your day with a morning ritual. Celebrate your body, whether it's with dance, deep breathing, meaningful stretching, or engaging movement. Spend a minimum of five minutes bringing your body to life. After all, it's only five minutes.

You can personalize this routine to best suit your channel. Use it to create energy that will propel you through your day and help you navigate it with a positive approach.

Are you a 10 in the morning? Likely not, but this type of routine can start your body and mind moving in that direction. Carpe Dime!

Somatic Movement

A method of moving the body I've been exploring recently is somatic movement. It's a different way of checking in and connecting with the body, and it's gentle, so it's ideal for those with limited mobility or chronic pain.

Somatic means "of or relating to the living body," and somatic movements are done "with the intention of focusing on the internal experience of the movement rather than the external appearance or result."[24] They are performed slowly to let the nervous system adjust, they require internal focus and attention to learn how the body responds, and they are exploratory—testing the level of fear, pain, or pleasure pleasure that each movement brings to our body. It's all about the process, which can be a new way of thinking for people who work out with concrete goals, and about the quality of the movement, not the quantity. These characteristics make somatic movement easy to do wherever you are and however much time you have.

Somatic movements also have a meditative quality that makes them a natural stress and tension reliever, and somatic psychotherapy can be used to explore more of the mind/body connection and how trauma has created muscle tension, digestive problems, sleeping problems, and respiratory problems, among other symptoms.

The following is an example of somatic movement. I've included many more exercises in the workbook section for you to do as part of your B.F.D. training (see pages 146–148).

Somatic Standing Awareness: This is a good start to somatic movement. Stand up straight with your feet rooted to the floor and notice how your feet grip the floor. Try to contract and release those foot muscles. Take deep breaths and notice how your abdominal muscles expand and contract, bringing awareness to how this breathing makes you feel. Finally, scan your body from top to bottom, noticing how your different muscles feel, and pay particular attention to any areas of tension so you can focus on them.

Somatic movement is a relatively new practice in Western cultures, but it draws on ancient practices from other cultures. Studies have shown that increasing awareness of posture and movements can help make specific changes in body language to reduce unwanted emotions and promote a more positive emotional experience.[25] It can also help people expand their movement and increase bodily self-awareness to treat chronic low back pain.[26]

The Body, in Brief

If you take anything away from this chapter, it should be that the mind follows the body. We humans are tremendously powerful creatures, and we have subtle ways we can harness the power of the body and increase our energy and capacity.

When you're feeling down or stressed or nervous, or if you just want to bump yourself up the Dime scale, do one or more of the following. You'll be surprised at the quick and positive changes, and soon you'll be doing them as a matter of course.

- Stand tall and look to the rooftops
- Show the world your teeth
- Breathe into your belly
- Believe in your voice
- Move, and do it joyfully

As the title of the John Mayer song says, "Your Body Is a Wonderland"—appreciate it and treat it that way!

CHAPTER THREE

Focus

NOW THAT YOU have your body sending signals of strength, joy, and calm to your brain, let's take that oh-so-complicated organ and find ways to channel your positivity and focus your thinking.

I'll preface this chapter by saying that our minds are often overwhelmed and overworked, especially as we deal with the fallout of the pandemic and the devastating world events that come at us fast and furious. If you can access it, professional counseling can be incredibly helpful when it comes to gaining self-knowledge and sorting through the tangle of emotions the world can trigger. Mental health support and therapy can be a lifesaver.

This chapter isn't a replacement for professional help, and it's not a panacea for all your mental health challenges. It's a guide to help you look at your life through a new lens and find a way to be more proactive and conscious in the way you perceive and interact with the world around you, instead of being reactive to events beyond your control.

In this chapter you will find ways to reframe your thinking in your daily life and approach your emotional landscape just a little differently so that you're a little lighter, a little more in control of your moods, and a little more intentional in your thoughts. That in turn will influence how you manage, and increase, your energy.

One of the most important decisions you'll ever make is what to focus on, and that's a choice you make all day, every day. It sounds overwhelming, but you can choose what you give your attention to, and it will soon become second nature.

You already have the power of focus. Let's learn how to use it!

Worry and the Body

Think about how you feel when something makes you anxious. You sweat, your pulse quickens, you feel sick, you get a headache. I always say the symptoms of anxiety are basically everything.

I mean, look at this list of symptoms:

- Feelings of shock, anger, sadness, or fear
- Disbelief or denial
- Emptiness or numbness
- Difficulty sleeping or nightmares
- Changes in appetite and energy

- Headaches, stomach problems, or body pains
- Worsening of mental or chronic health conditions
- Increased use of alcohol, tobacco, and other substances[1]

These symptoms aren't arbitrary. They are the fallout from our sympathetic nervous system having been continually or routinely engaged in a fight-or-flight response. Our response to external stress is universal and involuntary. Being in a state where our heart rate and breathing are rapid, our muscles are tense, and our senses are heightened is seriously detrimental if it lasts for too long. Anxiety is not only detrimental to our physical health; it also saps our emotional strength, willpower, and ability to be in control of our circumstances.

It can also hasten the aging process and be a precursor to serious disease on a cellular level.

"Living with stressors is unavoidable in the life of organisms and cells, thus the cells have to divert at least some of their resources from other pathways, to deal with the consequences of stressors," say the researchers Borut Poljšak and Irina Milisav. "Our cells are well adapted to exposure to a mild stress for a short time. In contrast there are potentially serious consequences of exposure to the prolonged stress. Cellular stress can at least contribute to, or even trigger, many diseases and malignant transformations and has an important role in aging."[2]

And while this information is useful, and I hope helpful, it can also be damaging, as when we talk or read about anxiety and the way it manifests itself, we interact more with our worries, which in itself can trigger our stress response and leave us feeling even worse.

It goes without saying, then, that breaking the cycle of anxiety can be extremely difficult. And no one is immune. I live in that cycle more than I care to admit. When my daughter coughs in her sleep, I immediately worry, so I go to WebMD and feel even worse. I can find any number of rare and deadly diseases that cause a cough. I might even invent a few of my own. Then I call someone and tell them all about it. My dialogue is full of that worry, and the cycle continues, feeding itself.

Not all worry is negative, though. Some is there to move us into action and bring awareness to something that needs our attention. In the case of my daughter, my worry about one random cough is simply a small thing that becomes giant because of my focus.

Whatever I focus on I will feel, and whatever I focus on I will find.

· · · · · · · · · · · ·

Whatever I focus on I will feel, and whatever I focus on I will find.

· · · · · · · · · · · ·

In worry and anxiety lives another opportunity for us to practice self-awareness and learn to mitigate the harm that external factors may be doing to us. External factors offer us a chance to see how our thoughts have power, and how that power can be turned around and used positively. If we recognize anxiety and can name it, we can use some of our techniques to ease it. We can then take back control and move up the Dime scale.

Our physical cells are affected by our thoughts. When we're stressed and burdened with anxiety, we're weakened and easily pushed around or manipulated. When we think of something that makes us feel inspired, we are much stronger and grounded in our resolve. The circumstance of our reality is the same in both instances; only our thoughts and where we've placed our focus have changed.

Research has shown that even the simple act of nodding (positive) your head versus shaking it side to side (negative) can increase athletic performance, particularly when done in conjunction with encouraging self-talk.[3]

Conversely, anxiety can cause muscle weakness. The symptoms of fight-or-flight cause muscle fatigue through shallow or quickened breathing, muscle tension, a change in blood flow to the extremities, high blood pressure, or a combination of any or all of these. Feeling weak then causes more anxiety and produces another negative feedback loop in the body. This can make you hyperaware of what's happening to your body, leading you to believe the muscle weakness is much more acute than it actually is.[4]

I do an exercise with my corporate clients where I have a volunteer stand up with their arms straight out at their sides. I ask them to think of something that causes them stress and anxiety. It usually doesn't take long for them to come up with something. Then, while they are in that mindset, I try to push their arms down. Guess what? Their arms collapse to their side with little resistance.

What does this mean on a grand scale? Imagine what the repeated tension and resistance you feel, all caused by your own focus, is doing to your overall health.

I then ask the same person to adopt the same pose with their arms, but this time I tell them to think of something that makes them feel excited, happy, inspired, or empowered—and ideally all four. When I try to push their arms down in this state, it's almost impossible to move them. It's like the world's easiest magic trick. You should see the look on their faces.

When we think of something that makes us feel inspired, we are much stronger and grounded in our resolve. And all that has changed is what we have chosen to think about and focus on.

When I tell people about this exercise, they typically don't believe me until they do it themselves. You might not believe me. Try it with a friend who doesn't mind you pushing on them a little, and then reverse positions. You'll be amazed at the difference when you switch your mind's focus from negative emotions to the things that bring you joy.

I saw a similar effect as a personal trainer. People who were working out while feeling down or focusing on their problems were not reaping the benefits of the exercise and were more likely to injure themselves. Granted, this is anecdotal evidence, and I didn't quantify it or test it scientifically, but after many years in the gym and working with hundreds of clients, it's a conclusion I'm comfortable arriving at.

I learned that if you choose to feed the soul with positive thoughts while also moving the body, you'll have a much more productive workout and be less likely to pull a muscle and end your session prematurely.

What's Your Frequency?

Imagine getting a flat tire while you're on your way to a party. You don't need to be there at a certain time, but you are nonetheless looking forward to getting there.

Take a moment and examine the feelings that arise in you.

Are you in a detailed negative state? Did your mind start spinning through all the problems the flat would create? Were you in a neutral state? Did you see the problem for what it was and simply get on with your day? Or were you in a detailed positive state? Did you think about the positives that could arise from the flat, like a cool rental car? Or the satisfaction of replacing the flat yourself? Or experiencing the kindness of strangers who might stop and help you?

Just as you can train your body in sport-specific skills, you can train your mind to focus on an ideal situation. But why is that important?

Your brain is like a radio, and you feel what you choose to tune in to. If you're just listening to the static of worries and doomsday scenarios, your mind will stay there and you'll get stuck in the spiral of negativity, in a state of discomfort or despair.

When you're confronted with a problem, do you listen to your brain broadcasting worst-case scenarios or best-case scenarios? The human tendency is to listen to the old favorites playlist, which is 95 percent worrying about what could go wrong and 5 percent coming up with ideas or solutions.

We need to update our station selection and reverse that tendency. It's not going to happen immediately, but it's a conscious decision you can make the next time you're listening to your mind and it's telling you how everything

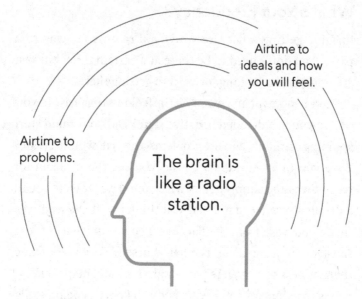

Airtime to ideals and how you will feel.

Airtime to problems.

The brain is like a radio station.

could go wrong. It's a chance to push yourself and flex your mental strength.

Tune into a higher frequency—Channel 10 or Radio Dime—and you will have more energy and ability to accept and work through a challenge. Even if you manage to move from detailed negative up to generally positive, you're on the way to detailed positive. Ultimately, you should try to be at 95 percent solutions and ideal scenarios and 5 percent worry. (95.5 on your Dime dial!)

Remember, whatever we focus on, we will feel.

New Ideals

There's an example from my past life I like to use to illustrate why focusing on ideal scenarios is so important.

I was living in New York City and had to get from my place in Manhattan to JFK airport to catch a flight so I could teach a workshop in Nova Scotia the next morning. Feeling confident I knew the vagaries of Big Apple traffic and could get there in plenty of time to enjoy my preflight drink from a large, Seattle-based coffee chain, I gave myself two hours to get there in an Uber. It was less than 20 miles. I was Diming, listening to my tunes and imagining returning to my humble Maritime roots as a successful, big city woman.

Then I checked my Uber app and saw the estimated time of airport arrival ticking up and up and up. I was going to get there much closer to the final boarding call than I'm comfortable with. I am not a late person. I love to be early (and I love my Seattle-based coffee chain drink).

You have probably been in a similar situation and can imagine how I was feeling. I let myself go down the rabbit hole of the problem and pictured everything that could possibly go wrong. I was worried I'd miss the flight, there wouldn't be another one, I'd have to pay for a new flight, I wouldn't arrive in time for the workshop, I'd have to sleep at the airport, the client would be angry, they'd have to cancel the workshop, and I'd be on the hook for reimbursing everyone. Or, simply, everyone would hate me. That might be a little extreme, but that's the power of negative focus.

Imagine now how that manifested itself physically as I ran down the laundry list of negative scenarios. My heart was racing and my breath was short. I was hot, restless, irritated, and uncomfortable. I was in survival mode, fight-or-flight, and not thinking clearly. My blood flow was not feeding my logical mind but was instead preparing to do battle or to flee.

While I was thinking this way, I didn't get to enjoy my music or being chauffeured to the airport. And if I had kept thinking that way, I would have shown up at the check-in desk wild-eyed and out of control. They would have seen me knocking down both babies and the elderly indiscriminately to clear my path because I had to make that flight! And clearly, the clerks at the check-in desk would feed off my energy and probably not be very helpful.

At that moment, in the back seat of the Uber on the way to the airport, I had neither made the flight nor missed it. The only thing within my power was what I chose to focus on.

Realizing that I was living a real-life example of the stuff I teach, I knew it was time to practice what I preach. So, I deliberately changed my focus. I chose to think about my ideal situation instead: that I'd arrive at the gate with enough time to get my special drink. I grew up in a tiny town and I'm still excited about fancy coffee, so I stopped looking at the app and focused on the coffee.

I imagined myself sitting at my gate, relaxed and slowly sipping my drink. And what happened? A feeling of joy washed over me. I started to enjoy the drive, and when I arrived at the airport, I was the kind, friendly Canadian I remained, even in the wilds of New York City. The airline staff were eager to help me, calling my gate to let them know I was on my way to catch my slightly delayed flight. And, yes, I got my coffee.

My ideal situation happened, and I enjoyed the whole experience. My body was at ease because I didn't waste time and precious energy living in my worst-case scenario.

We are all riding in a metaphorical Uber, starting to stress about something. What you choose to focus on and what you expect to happen will affect the way you show up at your destination. Choose the ideal situation, enjoy the ride, and get that coffee.

. . . .

What you choose to focus on and what you expect to happen will affect the way you show up at your destination.

. . . .

I told this story in Halifax, thinking it was a brilliant real-life illustration of the importance of focus. Someone in the crowd had doubts, of course.

A woman in a huge sea of people stopped me in the middle of my story and told me that she didn't want to envision the ideal scenario because if it didn't happen, she was setting herself up for disappointment. That didn't occur to me, because that's not the way I think, but she had me stumped, and I knew I had to take that kind of thinking into consideration.

I mulled it over, and in the middle of the night I woke up suddenly from a dead sleep with a perfectly Tweet-able, or should I say X-able, answer: "From every disappointment is a new ideal situation." Eureka!

That may not be exactly how I arrived at this response to her very reasonable concern, but it's how I choose to remember it.

I realized my story could have played out differently. I could have done all the focus work, been polite and calm, and still missed my flight and that moment of waiting to board with coffee in hand, secure in the knowledge that everything was going to plan. That moment I enjoy so much. However, if this were the case and my ideal scenario didn't materialize, thanks to the focus work I'd still be in a much better position to take the disappointment in stride and come up with my next ideal scenario.

Your ideal situation won't always happen, your worst-case scenario might even come to be, but you can pivot. You can find a new ideal situation based on new information or events and focus on that.

If I had missed the flight, maybe there would be another one I could catch soon after and maybe it would be empty, so they'd put me in first class. And maybe up there I'd sit next to someone who would turn out to be the love of my life or a great business connection who could change the course of my career.

At 20 years old, I would have cried to my mother on the phone, gotten deep into the detailed negative aspects of my story, and probably missed both my flight and new opportunities. It took me time and life experience to learn to refocus and redirect my thoughts.

• • • • • • • • • • •

From every disappointment is a new ideal situation.

• • • • • • • • • • •

This skill of shifting and settling my focus was particularly important during the pandemic.

With rules and expectations changing so rapidly, I was forced to continually reassess and refine my life and ideal scenarios. I was living in ways I couldn't have imagined just weeks or months prior—being isolated from loved ones, waking up by myself every day, moving back to Canada, and raising a newborn as a single mother, very much alone.

It was a daily struggle, and some days I lost the battle, but I was able to find new ideals and quickly adapt to them, and that may have saved me. It certainly kept me on my toes.

I look back now at the darkest time of my life, when everything changed in ways I couldn't control, and think about how it led me to where I am now, a very happy place. My daughter is healthy and growing, and my career has taken me back to my roots in athletics in ways I never would have imagined.

Sometimes difficult things happen for a reason that will become clear down the road. If you give yourself the space to accept them, better things can happen.

Prepare for the Good Stuff

Like the woman in Halifax, I have plenty of clients who disagree with me and say, "Jill, I have to think of the worst-case scenario so I can plan for it."

To them I say, "Think of the worst-case scenario 5 percent of the time." In fact, for preparation purposes, that is likely prudent. You can't turn a blind eye to the realities that confront you. You do need to have emergency preparedness planning, whether it's a first-aid kit in your car or a corporate plan of action for an unexpected public relations mess. But it's equally important to understand that if the worst case happens, you'll figure it out.

Conversely, if you spend all your time focused on the worst case (because you think that will somehow protect you from it happening), your physical self will feel the scenarios you are imagining and you'll show up like that, all under the guise of being prepared.

I want you to be prepared, but for the good stuff. Think of the ideal until you are 100 percent sure it won't happen, then come up with a new ideal situation. Trust yourself enough to know that you're resourceful and that you'll find a solution *if* a problem does arise.

I don't want to be too Pollyanna about this concept. There is suffering in the world, and I do know there are situations where it's almost impossible to find an ideal situation and hope. A serious illness, for example. When that's brought up by people I work with, I say that they can, and should, honor the sadness, disappointment, and anger that comes with those situations. I tell them to acknowledge and feel those emotions, then, after an appropriate period, think about what the next ideal is from that place.

You can adjust your sails in the storm and seek out smaller, achievable ideals. A new course of treatment, perhaps, or a new doctor who has insight or experience that will help. If nothing else, remind yourself that time spent with loved ones is ideal.

Our ability to turn a problem into an ideal scenario is one of our most powerful mental muscles. You have the opportunity to choose action versus reaction. You have the ability to take stock and be aware of a situation and then deliberately choose to shift it.

It takes practice, intention, and the ability to be aware of what you need in each moment. You need to recognize your worry and then apply this skill, not let the worry continue until it becomes all-consuming. This is a habit worth cultivating.

Focus on the Feeling, Not the Six-Pack

My personal training days were full of people who thought they'd be happy if they could get six-pack abs. Those, apparently, were the be all, the end all, and the key to unlocking all of life's joys. They believed suffering was necessary to get there, so they overexercised, underate, trained anxiously, and got injured.

Frustrated by setbacks, they sought comfort in eating cookies on the couch or drinking a six-pack, thereby setting themselves further back from what they had decided would be their most important achievement.

The other external validation I'd often encounter with clients was their choice of an arbitrary number on the bathroom scale. That gives all the power to the scale and takes away your own agency. Never mind that weight is rarely a reliable indicator of health, it's also a distant mirage that will rob you of your happiness for as long as that magic number eludes you. Many people feel that seeing a certain number on the scale will make them feel worthy, but if we can't create a feeling of worthiness from within first, no number on the scale will do it for us.

Now, I love a good goal or, more specifically, working toward that goal and knowing what I'm after, but consider what achieving that goal will make you feel. If it's happiness you're after, there are ways to get there without torturing yourself in the pursuit of a six-pack. If you can figure out how to be happy with yourself, you won't need that six-pack, and you might not even care if you have one or not.

Ironically, if you find happiness, you're more likely to achieve the six-pack goal. You'll have more energy to get out of bed and choose exercise, do it joyfully, and prepare and enjoy the right foods. So maybe the abs are a by-product; the life you're living is already joyous.

You can substitute the abs for just about anything in life—a better job, a bigger house—but the result is the same. And often people who do achieve one of these goals aren't satisfied for long, as they soon want the next shiny thing. This is an unfortunate consequence of Western consumer culture, and we all fall victim to it sometimes.

Money is another trap. Many people think they'll feel safe if they have a certain amount in the bank, so they chase money. That pursuit can be soul-crushing, and no amount of money can create a true sense of security if that condition doesn't already exist within you.

In examining your motivation, however, you get all the information you need. If it's safety and security you crave, then find a path to reaching that place inside yourself.

A real-life example from one of my clients will help drive this home. This client wanted to leave a big firm to start her own accounting business. At the big firm she felt overworked, stressed, and tired. She felt like she never had enough time, the clients were too demanding, and she wasn't doing the job right. So, she worked on the weekend to create her own client base, with the assumption that once she had 30 clients she would be in a comfortable enough space to start her new business.

She was near the beginning of this journey when we began working together. I asked her how many of her own clients she had, and she said nine. When I asked how it was going with them, she said she was always stressed and tired, the clients were demanding, and she felt like she didn't have enough time for them and wasn't doing her job right. She was frustrated, exhausted, and unmotivated.

She was bringing the same negative emotions she had with her job at the big firm to the work she was doing to leave that firm. If she continued on this path, she might leave the firm and be in a different office, but she'd be in the same place emotionally.

I encouraged her to examine what was truly driving her to want to leave the big firm. I encouraged her to refocus and explore what emotions she wanted her work to elicit.

My prescription was for her to step back and sort out the feelings she wanted to have, map out her ideal scenario, and then manage her energy to the point where she could receive energy that would match hers.

In the end, this client realized that there wasn't anything wrong with working at the big firm. What was making her unhappy was that she allowed herself to take on too much. Constantly feeling overwhelmed meant she felt she was not doing her job well, and that reduced her confidence in herself and her work. As a result, she felt drained and unfulfilled—and wanted to leave. She never said to her bosses, "I have too much work to do. It is unreasonable, and because

I can't give our clients the quality of service I know that I can deliver, I'm unhappy."

Sure enough, by focusing on what she wanted (feelings of happiness and confidence, as well as being a positive force for her firm and her clients), she identified the steps she needed to take (address the issues with her bosses) and acted accordingly. In the end, her bosses responded positively to her feedback and now she's excelling at work and in life. She didn't need to start her own firm (though if her bosses had responded differently, she may have wanted to), she simply needed to understand what it was she truly desired and then channel her energy into working toward that. It's not always the external thing that we really want. It's often the external thing that gives us insight into how we want to feel. But if we can start there—understanding how we want to feel—we then have the freedom to find those feelings without necessarily needing to achieve the external thing.

So, when you find yourself unhappy, or the next time you're beating the worry drum, here's a checklist for how to shift your focus and change the channel on your cranial radio:

- Write down and focus for two minutes on something that always makes you feel good. My little nephews often appear on my list.
- Once you start reaching a higher channel, examine the problem you are having from a new perspective, from an elevated position. We looked at the rooftops earlier. Let's stand on them now.
- Think about an exciting new ideal situation for the circumstance that's troubling you.

- Focus on the process, not the goal. Identify the steps you need to take, and embrace the journey that lies ahead.
- Practice the emotion you are seeking in the moment.

Focus, in Brief

You reap what you sow emotionally. It's cause and effect. If you plant corn, you get corn, and if you focus on worry, you can't hope to harvest joy. Bring attention to what you're focusing on, what you're planting and watering, because it will grow like a weed.

When you realize you've been giving too much attention to the negative, try to refocus and reframe it. Starve the negativity and feed the joy by finding moments of happiness and looking for new ideal situations.

If you find you continue to focus on things that bring you down—what's not working, what you don't have, a problem life has handed you—consider where your energy is going. My guess is that you're not spending it on new ideal situations or solutions, and when you're bogged down in the negative, you won't have the energy you need to find ways out. You only have low channel energy available to you, and that will keep you in your rut.

The channels of a problem and of a solution are very different. If you want to climb to a Dime, make the conscious decision to choose the solution channel. That's one of our superpowers we don't tap into enough.

Happiness hacks are everywhere if you look. I've spoken about the things in life we all have that make us smile. Choosing to focus on one of those, even briefly, will give you an immediate boost of energy and happiness.

Like many things I recommend, it's a nice little shortcut in your day that doesn't involve a grand effort or lifestyle change. Watch a cat video, try a toothy smile, dance like nobody's watching or everyone is, whichever you prefer.

Focus on that brief feeling of joy, not external validation or unachievable goals. Live in those little moments we can create. The more you welcome them, the more they will come.

I remember when it dawned on me that we're always on a journey, whether it's a ride share to an airport or a spiritual one. We naturally try to move from suffering to happiness, and I want to feel the excitement and positive emotions I imagine at the end of that road throughout the trip.

I found a way to enjoy my ride to JFK, and I've found ways to focus on the joys of my journey in life, bumps, setbacks, and all.

Once you get yourself to a higher channel, you'll have the energy and motivation you need to find new insights, ideas, and ideals. The problems you've been ruminating on will look different and become smaller.

And remember, whatever we focus on we feel, and whatever we focus on we find.

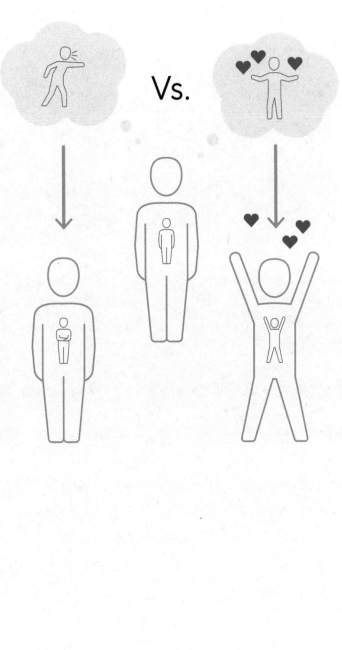

CHAPTER FOUR

Dialogue

AT ITS MOST simple, dialogue is the conversation you have with yourself, in your head—and sometimes with yourself out loud (don't worry, we all do it). Dialogue is also the conversation you have with the broader world about who you are.

Encompassed in dialogue are the ideas of visualization, manifesting, and positive thinking—ideas very much thrust into the mainstream by Rhonda Byrne and her best-selling books *The Secret* and *The Power*. While Byrne has received some criticism for the lack of scientific rigor in her assertions and for pushing unrealistic hope, to me, the fact they became such well-known books and concepts means they resonated with a wide audience—an audience who embraced the potential for positive changes within and in their personal and professional lives.

Now science is validating the power of belief and its ability to shape our reality. Research has shown that confident—even overconfident—people appear more socially skilled and competent. They're also more likely to notice and seek out opportunities because they believe they're capable and deserving of them. Similarly, people are more likely to live a healthy lifestyle if they believe they're capable of performing healthy behaviors and following through on healthy choices.[1]

Beliefs about your own basic character are especially powerful. In one study, children who were praised for being helpful—a characteristic versus a behavior—turned out to be more altruistic than children who were praised nonspecifically or not praised at all.[2] And in adults, shame as a self-belief has been shown to be a self-fulfilling prophecy by reducing the confidence needed to make any positive changes.

Shame, as opposed to guilt associated with an action, is a belief about yourself—that you're not enough. It may have been planted by a parent or a loved one, and over time it becomes part of your identity.

As defined by the writer and well-being expert Dr. Tchiki Davis of the Berkeley Well-Being Institute, shame "arises as a result of negative evaluations from others, even if we're just being ourselves. It's not so much that what we did that is bad, but that who we are is bad. As a result, we may feel small, worthless, or powerless. Over time, shame can lead to something called the 'internalized other'—an image or idea that someone disapproves of us. We may then hold negative evaluations of ourselves through the eyes of others."[3]

You retreat inward, believing you really aren't enough for certain people or situations. You find ways to prove to yourself that you're lacking and your actions reflect it. And in that state, the thought of seeking any sort of help seems like a failure waiting to happen. Surely you'll disappoint your therapist, your loved ones . . . yourself. And you're probably not worth helping. So you don't do anything, and there's shame in not making changes or having the strength to speak up. It's yet another shortcoming.

Fortunately, on the Berkeley Well-Being Institute website, Davis has methods of identifying shame and improving your self-esteem through shame-focused self-compassion, meditation, and visualization. If you recognize these feelings, you might want to look up her work.

Your beliefs also influence others. A well-known study involved male participants talking on the phone to female participants. They were told beforehand that the female participants they would be talking to were either attractive or unattractive. "Analysis of the recordings by outside observers showed that throughout the conversation, women perceived as more attractive came to behave in a more friendly and likeable way than those who were perceived as less attractive, suggesting that participants' expectations not only shaped their own perceptions of their conversation partner— they also seemed to elicit behavior that confirmed their expectations."[4]

In a romantic context, if one partner sees the other in an idealized light, the relationship tends to be healthier and last longer. The idealizer's belief alleviates insecurity and instills confidence in their partner, and these secure partners are more likely to act in generous and constructive ways. In contrast, those who perceive hostility or ill intentions in their partner are more likely to act in ways that prompt hostility or foster division.[5]

And while underlying health factors are beyond our control, one study showed that middle-aged adults who had a positive view of aging lived 7.5 years longer than those who had a negative one.[6] Other experiments have also proven that the placebo effect is real: just by believing we're being treated for a condition, our health can improve, based on patterns of brain activation and the release of dopamine.[7]

· · · · · · · · · · · ·

Your stories are not only reflecting the quality of your life, they're also *creating* your life.

· · · · · · · · · · · ·

The long and short of it is, your stories are not only reflecting the quality of your life, they're also *creating* your life. That sounds heavy, but the ability to harness the power of your dialogue is another superpower you can cultivate.

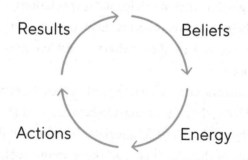

Your beliefs determine your energy, your energy leads to your actions, and those actions create results. Then those results reinforce your beliefs. Rinse and repeat.

It's a powerful, self-perpetuating circle.

Changing the Stories You Tell Yourself

If you want to change your path in life or change the energy you both give and receive, you need to change the stories you tell yourself.

Just like learning new habits with your body and focus, harnessing the power of your dialogue requires self-awareness and practice. With enough time, your dialogue can become a habit that takes on its own positive momentum.

It starts with your beliefs. A belief is a practiced thought, one you keep thinking to make it your truth, and if you think it long enough, it will start to spin your circle in whatever direction you send it.

The belief is the centrifugal force, sending your energy outward, leading to action and results. It's powerful, so use it wisely or it will work against you.

In addition to the studies cited at the beginning of this chapter, I have so many examples of this from my work with my clients. One particular client was sure her colleagues didn't like her and that became her belief, so when she went into work her energy was low and her actions were hesitant and awkward. As a result, people weren't comfortable around her, and this fed into her insecurity and belief that she was disliked. It was a circle that grew stronger over time, making it more and more difficult to break the cycle.

. . . .

Our thoughts are creating our reality all the time.

. . . .

We all contribute to our circles in all their aspects, so why not make each circle a positive, uplifting force? If you believe you're a good athlete, your energy will be up when you train, you'll train more often and at more intense levels, you'll likely enjoy training more, and then you'll get the results that prove you're a good athlete. And so your circle gets strengthened.

Our thoughts are creating our reality all the time. It's not magic. It's happening through this constant, often subconscious circle.

Once you recognize your circle(s), you want to be very conscious of what thoughts you're feeding them. A belief in yourself is one of the most important things to put into the circle—confidence in yourself and your ability will change the outcomes around you. Your energy will increase, your actions will become inspired, and your results will change.

A pop culture example of this very real phenomenon is the 2018 movie *I Feel Pretty*, starring Amy Schumer. Her character doesn't have a lot of self-belief and she's insecure about her appearance. Her energy isn't strong, and her life isn't going too smoothly or successfully as a result. Then she falls off her spin bike at SoulCycle and lands on her head. After the head injury she looks in the mirror and perceives perfection, even though nothing physical has changed.

Empowered by her newfound confidence, she's incredibly energetic and not afraid to take action when she never would have before. She gives her number to handsome strangers and goes for jobs she's not really qualified for. And she gets results. The more she finds success, the more her self-belief grows and gains momentum, and the circle feeds itself.

When a movie plot is based on the power of self-belief and positive broadcasting, you know the concept has reached critical mass. There's also plenty of hard science to back up the assertion.

One of the most interesting examples of that science is a study by Stanford University's Dr. Alia Crum. She gave two groups of individuals the same milkshake; one group was told it was a nutrient-dense milkshake, with high levels of sugar and fat, and the other group was told it was a diet shake. It was the exact same beverage, but blood tests showed the physiological results of each group responded to exactly what they believed they were drinking.[8]

This is fascinating research! It seems that it's not just what you eat, but also what you *believe* about what you eat. It's not just what you're doing, but also what you *believe* you're doing. These beliefs are, again, just practiced thought patterns in the mind, and the experiment is further proof that your psychology is closely linked to your physiology, and vice versa.

Another study by Dr. Crum, titled "Mind-set Matters: Exercise and the Placebo Effect," sought to investigate "whether the relationship between exercise and health is moderated by one's mind-set." This study involved a group of hotel cleaners who were on their feet for hours a day, getting in thousands of steps and using their upper bodies while they worked, but who did not perceive themselves to be exercising during their work day. They were separated into two groups, with one group told how many steps they were taking and the benefits of the exercise inherent in their work. None of the participants made any major changes to their habits, but the group that was informed about the positives of their job lost weight and had lower blood pressure and cholesterol.[9]

The power of our beliefs is life-changing, so it is crucial to question what you feed into your circle.

I love knowing that my physiology responds to my beliefs, and I want to speak kindly about and to myself and positively about my abilities.

You may have had a lifetime of self-doubt and negative self-talk. Now is the time to change that inner dialogue and start to create the story of a happier, healthier life.

Here's another way to think of it: There is soil inside your body. What seeds will you plant? How will you feed them? Let the good grow inside you through positive inner dialogue, which is completely within your control. Don't wait for outside actors or events to do that for you, or to plant poison seeds.

A quote from the fourteenth-century Persian poet Hafiz that I love offers yet another way to consider it: "What we speak becomes the house we live in."[10]

Be Your Best Friend

When I approach this topic with my clients, I find most believe their dialogue isn't too bad. "Isn't too bad" is not the same as being good, however.

For many, getting to the point where you're not hard on yourself all day is a great accomplishment and you can be proud of that, but there's room for improvement if you want to empower yourself and Dime it up.

Many adults don't nag or criticize themselves all day, but they're not compassionate with themselves either. The basis for many people's self-talk consists of the running lists of things they need to do and the reminders they give themselves. For many, the only time they engage in meaningful inner dialogue is when something goes wrong—and then they choose to be critical or cynical. However, with practice you can open yourself up to the many opportunities you have each day to speak to yourself lovingly and positively.

When I first started teaching people about dialogue, I suggested they always have an imaginary cheerleader by their side. They could then decide each day whether to speak negatively to themselves or have the cheerleader root them on. This, however, was too limiting. When you make a mistake, or something bad happens, the last thing you want is a cheerleader whooping it up on the imaginary sidelines of your emotional field.

I now like to send people away with the idea that their inner voice should be that of a supportive best friend. Instead of simply trying to cheer you on to excellence the way the cheerleader does, the supportive best friend is emotive, empathetic, and kind. This sort of self-talk is the kind that can really make a difference in terms of moving up the Dime scale toward a 10.

An internal conversation like "Jill, you have been working so hard. I see all you are doing, I am so proud of you, keep up the great work, one day at a time, you got this!" is self-validating, encouraging, loving, and practical. It is the kind of thing we all need to hear, and you can say it to yourself.

As Dr. Kristen Neff, a lead researcher in the area of mindful self-compassion, says, "With self-compassion, we give ourselves the same kindness and care we'd give to a good friend."

More compassion is what we all need, especially now, and that goes double for the conversation you're having internally.

Neff has created a self-compassion scale (scs) that gauges thoughts, emotions, and behaviors to measure components of self-compassion, including self-kindness, common humanity, and mindfulness. An increased scs has been shown to correlate with higher levels of income, fulfilling relationships, job satisfaction, better health overall, and less depression and anxiety.[11]

Imagine experiencing improvement in all those areas of your life as a result of just being kind to yourself. Mindful self-compassion is not ignoring the harsh realities of the world. It's compassionately acknowledging those things that we find difficult and being gentle with ourselves as we try to sort them out.

Neff developed a three-step process to help us get there:[12]

1 Identify how you are actually feeling in the moment.
2 Recognize how this is part of the human experience, understanding that you are not alone or strange to feel how you're feeling.
3 Speak to yourself like your best, most supportive friend would.

A good example, and one that I've lived through and spoken about already, is having a child with a cold during the pandemic. In those days, when my daughter had a runny nose, I worried about whether she had COVID-19, whether she could go to daycare, and what I'd do about work the next day, and so on. My imagination is very active, especially when it comes to my precious little baby.

To use Neff's model in my case:

1 **Identify how you are actually feeling in the moment.**

   I'm feeling anxious, stressed, and very worried. Concerned about my daughter's health and my work. I'll throw angry and resentful into the mix because I'm a solo parent and I have to sort it all out myself.

2 **Recognize how this is part of the human experience, understanding that you are not alone or strange to feel how you're feeling.**

   I realize every single parent, and every parent who's single, has felt this when they've had a sick child, particularly since mid-March 2020.

3 **Speak to yourself like your best, most supportive friend would.**

   The best, most supportive friend I have would say, "Jill, this is a lot. There is so much to think about these days, trying to keep everyone safe and still get work done. Take a deep breath. Your clients will understand if you need to postpone. You have a great doctor who's one call away if you get concerned."

When I go through this exercise with my clients, some imagine their best friend would say, "It's fine, you'll figure it out. It's nothing to worry about." That's not the most compassionate you can be for your best friends.

For many of us, our default is to just push through. Adding compassion for yourself, as you would for those closest to you, can change the game.

Unfortunately, compassion is sometimes hard to come by, so here is a list of compassionate phrases you can use if you are finding it hard to give yourself the kindness you deserve. It was compiled by the psychologist Catherine Moore.[13]

- I accept the best and worst aspects of who I am.
- Changing is never simple but it's easier if I stop being hard on myself.
- My mistakes just show that I'm growing and learning.
- It's okay to make mistakes and forgive myself.
- I am free to let go of others' judgments.
- It's safe for me to show kindness to myself.
- I deserve compassion, tenderness, and empathy from myself.
- I release myself with forgiveness from today and move forward with self-love to tomorrow.
- Every day is a new opportunity, I won't let self-doubt or judgment hold me back from the future.
- I forgive myself and accept my flaws because nobody is perfect.
- I'm not the first person to have felt this way, and I won't be the last, but I'm growing.

When you're learning to be compassionate with yourself, try this trick. It generates kindness, and I like to use it to help me be kinder to myself.

When you're feeling scared or anxious, I'm hoping you have a person in your life you can call to vent to or seek advice from. Now, imagine you've had a tough time and you're going to call that person. Before you pick up the phone, think about what you want to hear. What will make you feel better in that situation?

Now ask yourself, why do you need someone else to tell you that?

We work so hard to get what we want from others— attention, acknowledgment, and validation, to name only a few. Why is that? Why wait for others to give us what we need?

When I get stressed or angry about something, I usually call my mother. There's always something I want to hear, and, depending on what state she's in, she may or may not be able to say it to me. Instead of leaving that to chance and the whims and moods of my mom, whom I love dearly, I've learned to ask myself what it is I hope she will say before I call her. I then say it to myself.

Then, when I do call, there's less pressure on our conversation because I've already begun to soothe myself.

The next time you feel like reaching out for positive reinforcement, figure out what you want or need to hear and try saying it to yourself. The answers are inside you, and the guidance you can give yourself as your best, most supportive friend can be transformational.

You can start by asking yourself regularly, "What is it that I need to hear right now?" Don't even wait for times of trouble. Do it often. It's good practice. Sometimes just thinking about what we need, even without coming to a conclusion, is enough to change our frame of mind. Sometimes we struggle express our needs fully, and that is bound to lead to disappointment if we outsource our need for self-compassion to others.

Try some encouraging self-talk and speak to yourself lovingly, with respect and kindness. By empowering yourself in this way, you become more self-sufficient, self-soothing, and self-advising. And you're always available.

Be Your Most Valuable Teammate

Similar to bringing along a compassionate best friend, sometimes I like to treat my inner dialogue as if I were a teammate with my body. After all, your mind and body are teammates—without the body, the mind wouldn't accomplish much, and without the mind, the body is also pretty useless.

The trouble is, we often speak to our body like we're not teammates with the same goal, more like we're on opposing teams or, worse, bitter rivals.

I think about this most in the gym or other fitness settings. People usually go to the gym to change or fix what they don't like about themselves; they walk in already engaged in an internal struggle. This creates tension in the body and can lead to illness and even disease, and it's definitely not going to help you achieve your goals.

When I played sports, one thing I would always say to my teammates was "Right idea," even if the execution was wrong. You want to support your teammates no matter what, just as you want to affirm yourself at all times.

I notice this a lot in my tennis community as well. I go to group lessons, and I've been playing with the same group of women, most of whom are older than me, for a few years. Some of them speak horribly to themselves, nattering the whole time, "Oh, I shouldn't have done that!" or "Nice hit, Sally!" (Imagine the last one dripping in sarcasm.)

I've also noticed that the ones who are hardest on themselves tend to be hard on the rest of us when we're knocking the ball back and forth too. I can't imagine that makes for a very fun trip to the courts. I know I don't take an hour out of my day to drive to the tennis dome to get cranky with myself and those around me.

When I play, I try to say things like, "Jill, let yourself learn." Or I remind myself to take a deep breath. Or I go with the old favorites, "Practice makes perfect" or "One shot at a time."

You don't learn anything when you're uncomfortable, and when you're hard on yourself, there's no way you can be comfortable.

Imagine how nice it would be as you go through an average day if there were no internal struggle between you and you, but instead you and you worked together as teammates toward the common goals of support, growth, and happiness. Imagine the energy you'd have.

Make sure you're on the same team as your body. Walk into a room and say, "We're on the same team! We want the same thing!"

That's going to create harmony within your body, and a harmonious team is a successful one.

Outside Reflects Inside (and Back Again)

I once had a fitness client who was put together and pristine, everything about her was just so. I felt like I had to get all done up for our appointments. She would comment on the people around us in an unkind way, and I felt pretty judged too.

I dreaded those sessions, but then I began to realize the person she was most judgmental of was herself, and I started to have more compassion for her. I imagine it's very hard to be inside her head. Her outward pettiness reflected her internal struggle.

If you want to change either the external or internal, you can use the other to affect change. If my client had learned to speak nicely to herself, she would have started to find the positive things about the people around her. Or she could have spoken nicely to the people around her, and in turn she would have started to notice the things about herself that she appreciated.

Do you find yourself impatient with others? If so, you're likely impatient with yourself. Before you can soften yourself to others, you need to be kinder and more loving to yourself. As Carl Jung famously said, "Everything that irritates us about others can lead us to an understanding of ourselves."[14]

Encountering an annoyance or frustration in life can be a learning experience. It often brings awareness to a situation you're experiencing on the inside. Recognizing and finding a solution to the reason you feel the emotion within yourself will begin to dissolve the issue you're experiencing with others.

Everyone you meet can be a mirror. They're showing you your weak spots, the places that need to be healed. For instance, a common relationship issue for people who felt abandoned by their parents (or who were actually abandoned by their parents) is choosing partners who are distant or unfaithful. It's subconsciously comforting to return to patterns you recognize and to prove yourself "right" by illustrating to your inner-self that people close to you are unreliable or untrustworthy. However, herein lies a tremendous opportunity to recognize your patterns and show yourself some love and understanding for past trauma.

No matter what patterns you are perpetuating, you can forgive yourself and know you're ready to heal.

The mirror can also be tremendously positive. When we learn to forgive and love ourselves, we can love and forgive others. When we get to that place, we can observe negative qualities in others without judgment or being triggered, and we can keep ourselves above the fray—we won't feel the need to engage in the drama or negativity.

And when we reach that place of acceptance, understanding, and love, we see it in others and draw them into our circle. When we focus on the light within, we can bring out the light in others.

. . . .

"Love is like a mirror. When you love another you become his mirror and he becomes yours . . . And reflecting each other's love you see infinity."[15] **—LEO BUSCAGLIA**

. . . .

One of my clients who was very health conscious offers another example of our outside reflecting in. She was always really hard on her husband about what he was eating, which told me that was how she spoke to herself about food. It wasn't actually about him. If she wanted to feel better about herself, and have a healthier relationship, she could have started to be kinder to him. In turn, she'd be kinder with herself. Or if she were softer with herself, eventually she would be gentler with him. Either way, he would be far more likely to change his eating habits because the push to do so would come from a more loving place.

On the flip side, Abbie, my favorite yoga teacher in New York City, has a twin sister. Both women have grown children who are all artistic, creative, and successful. I asked the twins what messaging they repeated to their children when they were young that might have helped them get to where they are in adulthood. After some consideration, they told me they affirmed them constantly—praising them, noticing what they were doing, and being enthusiastic about their activities.

I take a lot of Zoom classes with Abbie, and I've noticed that she spends time with each and everyone's little window and gives them positive affirmation.

"Beautiful backbend, Michael!"

"Wow, Alexandra, that is a thing of beauty!"

"Ty, aspirational!"

No wonder I like taking Abbie's classes so much! She is a confident, powerful woman, and I'm sure she gives herself the same healthy affirmations.

Abbie's inspiration can be a nice entry point for your B.F.D. dialogue. Start by affirming others around you. We notice people doing good things and often stay quiet. Start to speak up! Go out of your way to compliment people and watch how it uplifts not only them but you too.

Be your own cheerleader too. See how it pumps you up and increases your glow. If you're single (and you don't want to be), a great start before you hit the dating scene would be to explore your inner dialogue and get that in harmony. You'll see how it draws people to you.

That magnetism also works in professional situations. When you're in harmony and exude confidence and positive energy, you'll see results in your career.

Speak to Yourself in the Third Person

You may have noticed in the self-talk examples I've provided, I sometimes use my name when I speak to myself. There is a good reason for this, as Ethan Kross brilliantly points out in his book, *Chatter: The Voice in Our Head, Why It Matters, and How to Harness It.* Kross talks about using your first name when you speak to yourself as a way to interrupt your dialogue pattern. He says that the *reflexive* part of the brain, which is in charge of survival and is known as the lizard brain because it's not as developed or evolved, is the more critical and negative part of the brain. The *reflective* part, in the prefrontal cortex, is more intentional and positive.

In an experiment at the University of Michigan, Kross gave participants five minutes to prepare a speech. Half were told to refer to themselves in the first person, using "I," and half were told to use the second person, calling themselves "you," or to use their names. The former had more anxiety, while the latter displayed more confidence. When rated by those who listened to the speeches, those who used their first names were given a higher score in their overall performance.[16]

Using "I" in self-talk triggers the lizard brain and equates a problem with a threat. This part of the brain is lightning-fast and spontaneous. It's a hard-wired, survival voice that tends to be critical and negative and can lead to anxiety, depression, self-doubt, and self-sabotage.

For example, instead of saying, "I don't understand these edits, I must not be a very good writer," I might say, "Jill, you're a smart person and a capable writer, you'll talk to your editor and get clarity."

Kross is quoted as saying, "I try to coach myself using my own name. Trying to think through the problem that way helps me be level-headed and objective."[17]

Self-talk from the prefrontal cortex involves higher levels of intentional and positive thought. This compassionate voice is a learned skill that activates your "thinking brain," countering the lizard brain's fear and negativity. It unlocks healthier feelings like confidence, calmness, clarity, and joy. Using the third person activates the reflective part of the brain, which is particularly helpful in a world full of discord and uncertainty. The reflective part of the brain sees a problem as a challenge, instead of a threat, and uses reason to regulate emotions.

"The mind is flexible, if we know how to bend it," Kross says. "If you have a fever, you can take something to bring it down. Likewise, our mind has a psychological immune system: We can use our thoughts to change our thoughts—by adding distance."[18]

Several studies support Kross's assertions. A Michigan State University study looked at brain scans of people who used third-person self-talk, also known as distanced self-talk, and found that those people were better at regulating emotional distress when viewing disturbing images and that any anxiety eased when they referred to themselves in the third person. Another study, this one conducted at the University of Toronto, showed that using a calm, reflective inner voice while performing tasks gave participants self-control and prevented the reflexive brain from making rash decisions and mistakes. It further showed that greater self-control was exercised when participants could talk themselves through tasks.[19]

In the heat of the moment, the lizard brain often wins. Your challenge is to step outside and see that from a distance. Try to separate yourself from this ego challenge and look at the triggering event dispassionately. Take a wider perspective for some clarity, and give yourself a bit of understanding and compassion.

Exercising self-control in this way and becoming a detached observer of your own life, particularly at times of heightened emotion, isn't easy, but it produces great results. Here are some tips to get you started.

- Internally refer to yourself by your first name to remove the lizard brain's egocentrism and untangle yourself from it ("Jill, I know you're angry that the lawyers are misrepresenting the facts, but that's their job. You won't change them.").
- Use your own name to give greater power to your compliments (instead of "I really kept it together when triggered today," say "Jill, you were a rock today, the very picture of composure!").

- Think of yourself as the narrator of your own story instead of the actor, especially in difficult circumstances—it creates distance instead of immersion in the problem, allowing you to apply more thoughtful reasoning to the situation.

- Name negative or unpleasant parts of yourself to separate yourself from them ("My Timekeeper won't leave me alone today. She's upset that I'm running five minutes late.").

- Name your emotions and speak to them ("What's up, Rage? Why do you feel the need to create elaborate revenge scenarios?").

- Be compassionate when speaking to your lizard brain ("I understand you doubt that you can write an entire book and will be judged harshly when it comes out, but you have a lot of interesting experiences to draw upon and a lot of help along the way.").

Soothe Your Inner Child to Calm the Outer Adult

We have a kid in our belly and an adult in our throat. When we're losing control of our emotions, it's usually our inner child who's upset. That kid holds on to our past experiences. They recall times when we weren't always safe, when our needs weren't met or there wasn't someone looking out for us. The unsafe-feeling child is screaming and needs our inner adult to soothe them.

Much like a living child who is losing control and whose concerns you can't minimize by telling them that everything is fine or by distracting them with an iPad or a snack, your inner child needs to be nurtured, not ignored.

As adults, we often dismiss or diminish the problems of our inner child instead of honoring them, and there are so many ways to distract yourself, most of which are unhealthy. (Think screen time and snacks, the same distractions many of us offer to children. But there is no judgment here. Sometimes you just need to calm the waters before you can dive under them.)

The way you should ideally speak to a real child—validating their concerns and providing them with comfort and compassion—is the same way you should also speak to yourself. Show your inner child the love and compassion you crave. Say something like, "Jill, I know that, in the past, you weren't always looked after, or you didn't feel safe, or you didn't feel like there was an adult you could trust to look after you. But there's an adult present who sees you, cares about you, and is going to make sure that you are very well taken care of and you get what you need. You can rest easy, little one. I got you."

That's very soothing for both a real child and an inner child.

Speaking of adult children, before I moved to New York, I moved in with my parents for a month. Admittedly, I was anxious. I wondered what I'd do during the day and in the evening and how my new living arrangements would impact my very established routines. It also sent me right back to how I felt when I last lived with them, a lifetime ago, before I became a mature, confident adult. I was worried we'd clash as we did when I was a teen and that being in close proximity would test our patience and strain our relationship. There were also some feelings of shame for "taking a step backward" by moving home. I felt embarrassment when I told people what I was doing.

My tendency in those circumstances is to overplan, so I started to fill in a calendar with what I would do day by day to keep myself occupied. But I stopped myself. I reminded myself that I hadn't stayed there in a while, so I didn't really know what it would be like to be living at home. I also quickly realized that it was my kid within who was freaking out, because being under my parents' roof again felt like a regression to childhood.

Further, I realized I had to let my ego go and admit that I was accepting help in order to move forward. I was grateful I had the option to move in with them, and when I thought about my situation more, I believed our positive relationship likely wouldn't be strained because I wasn't the same kid who moved out all of those years ago.

I opted to trust that adult Jill could utilize her resources and ensure that I would get what I needed. I could tell my little kid, "Jill, I know you're worried about your routines, but I'm right here and I'm caring for you and I'm going to make sure things work out."

We have to create harmony for our child and our adult. Elizabeth Gilbert, the author of *Eat, Pray, Love*, put it very well in a podcast when she spoke about fear. She said fear is like a kid who is screaming (I picture it taking place on a road trip) and that you can say to the kid, "Your emotions are totally valid and I hear them. However, I'm going to strap you into your car seat where you'll be safe. You're not going to drive and you're not going to navigate, but you will be safe."[20]

(I can recommend Gilbert's *Big Magic: Creative Living Beyond Fear*. It's a guide to leading a more fulfilled life by making creativity a part of your daily existence and how to access your inner creativity.)

Let your fear and your little kid be welcome in every situation. Why? Because you know you're not going to let them be in control. Remember that you're the adult, you have agency, and your future self is at the wheel of the car, looking forward to what's next. Your inner child is tucked safely in the back seat.

I personally take everything to the extreme, so I have a vivid picture of a road trip with my current self and my future self in the front as driver and navigator, looking back at little me and saying, "Look who's here! We're all fine!" It's a fun family adventure.

What's Your Primary Statement? (Meet It with a Power Statement)

Your primary statement (or question) is what you're telling (or asking) yourself all the time, consciously or not. It plays on repeat in your head, and because you are so used to it, you don't even realize it's part of your inner dialogue.

We all have a primary statement (or question). It's something we go to when challenged, and it's the way we justify the things that happen to us (often only the bad things). I find it has the flavor of either shame or blame. People with a blame question or statement tend to be a little more intense.

When things don't go your way, your blame statement (or question) is the conclusion you come to. They look something like this:

"Something's wrong with me."

"I'm not good/talented/rich/attractive/smart enough."

"Why me?"

"What am I doing wrong?"

"What will other people think?"

"Why do I have to do it all?"

These statements (or questions) create a target around you and tend to perpetuate the narrative of your life. The more you say these things, the more the experiences of the past are repeated, and these patterns, like the circles, feed themselves and grow in power.

Think about the last time something didn't go according to plan, maybe at work or in a relationship. What was your immediate conclusion? What was the first thing you said to yourself?

You need to understand the primary statement playing in your head. Take the time to figure it out, then find the opposite statement to counteract it. This is your power statement, and it will calm your whole nervous system when you find the one that fits.

I can think of a few examples. I had a client in New York who was a producer, a busy mom with two kids. When challenged, her go-to question was "Why do I have to do it all?"

That held a touch of blame, and she was super fiery, to the point that you would probably not jump to help her. And no matter what her partner did, it would never be enough because she had that story locked in and running. She had to do it all.

It took some time, but we were able to get to a place where she changed her statement to "People are ready and willing to support me." Once she was able to take that power statement on board, she was much calmer.

I had another mom with two kids who lived close to her in-laws. Her primary question was "What will other people think?"

She was upset that she was always being judged by her in-laws on her parenting. "What will other people think?" created a target on her back that invited unwanted feedback. It made her less confident, and people were drawn to her unspoken statement, giving them permission to be less than kind and compassionate.

We found her two power statements: "I do what's right for me" and "I approve of myself and that's enough." They helped her deflect blame and replace it with affirmation.

You will always seek out evidence to prove what you're saying or feeling. That's confirmation bias—the tendency to search for, favor, and use information that confirms your existing views. Your confirmation bias rejects new information that contradicts your beliefs. Like shifting from detailed negative to detailed positive, learning how to resist your confirmation bias is a big reason you need to turn your primary question into a power statement. By identifying and using a power statement, you increase your agency and confidence instead of convincing yourself there's something fundamentally wrong with you.

Here are just a few of the powerful ways positive affirmations have been proven beneficial:

- Self-affirmations have been shown to lower stress that causes illness.[21]
- They can be effective in leading people to increase their physical activity and exercise.[22]
- They can assist in weight loss and reduce health risks.[23]
- They can make us less likely to ignore warning messages about harmful health effects, such as those on cigarette packages, and be more receptive to healthy lifestyle choices.[24]
- They have been linked positively to academic achievement by lessening or reversing GPA decline in students who don't feel they belong in college.[25]

Isn't it fascinating how a little self-imposed positivity can make such a huge difference?

I used to wonder what was wrong with me, or what I had done wrong, when things didn't go my way. I blamed myself. But then I realized I needed to find my own power statement. The one that felt right to me was "I'm in the right place, at the right time, doing the right things, and the right things are coming to me." And I repeated it over and over until I truly believed it. It became part of me.

In the workbook (see pages 163–165), I'll walk you through an exercise to help you find your power statement. For now, here are some that you might want to refer to as you think about your life:

"I'm already loved, and I'm already chosen."
"People are ready and willing to support me."
"No rush. I'm being in the moment."
"It's about my energy, not my effort."

"I approve of myself and that's enough."

"All I need is within me now."

"I trust the timing of my life."

"I'm worthy of receiving good things."

Make your power statement an incantation. Just as you're in control of your energy, so too are you in control of your power statement's message. You're no longer open to hearing opinions; your opinion is the only one that matters. And if you can have a power statement that counteracts your primary statement when it arises, you'll feel your nervous system relax.

Finding your primary statement (or statements, for some of us) is crucial if you are going to move up the Dime scale to be closer to 10 more consistently. Uncovering it can be harder than finding your power statement, though. Your primary statement was likely formed in your youth and has likely followed you throughout your life. It was probably the same in high school as it is, or as it will be, in your 30s or 50s. Your primary statement is deep-rooted and will be difficult to remove. But I assure you, once you find it, the effort of digging up those roots and planting a new thought in the form of a power statement will be well worth it. With enough practice and repetition, eventually, and especially when under duress, your primary statement will be entirely replaced by your power statement. And on the day that happens, you'll be Diming no matter what comes your way.

I recommend to my clients that once they find their primary statement and identify their power statement, they start repeating the statement out loud for two minutes a day. Try to ensure the subconscious primary statements or questions don't creep in. Don't give them the mental space. Power them out. Once that exercise is comfortable, I suggest they increase it. Eventually, you will hum it to yourself while doing the groceries or cleaning the bathroom. You'll know it is getting locked in when you are also able to unconsciously repeat it when life is difficult.

It has been proven that with enough time and effort, we can rewire our subconscious programming. There is MRI evidence suggesting that the ventromedial prefrontal cortex—the part of the brain involved in positive valuation and self-related information processing—becomes more active when we consider our personal values.[26] So, say goodbye to your primary statement. Without it you can welcome a new you, full of confidence and power.

Here are some more power statements for you to consider. Which ones speak to you?

- I choose to be happy.
- I'm gifted with and surrounded by amazing friends and family.
- I opt to rise above negative feelings and ditch negative thoughts.
- I am resilient, strong, and brave.
- Nobody but me decides how I feel.
- I am in charge of my thoughts, and I don't judge myself.
- I accept and love myself, thoroughly and completely.
- By being myself, I bring happiness to other people.

- My goals and desires are as worthwhile as everybody else's.
- I'm fine with who I am, and I love who I'm becoming.
- Through my contributions, I make positive changes to the world.
- My body is amazing just the way it is, and I accept myself this way.
- Whenever I fall down, I get back up again.
- I am a quick, capable learner.
- I am unique and beautiful.
- If a few people don't accept me, I'm fine with that.
- I forgive others for sometimes doing the wrong thing, and I forgive myself when I do the same.
- Whatever difficulties come my way, I have the power to overcome them.

Dialogue, in Brief

Dialogue can be difficult, whether it's exploring the stories you tell yourself and the world or seeking your primary statement (or question). It's delving into deep parts of your psyche and soul, but I've felt the results and I've seen the results and I know it's worth it.

If you notice there are patterns in your relationships, issues that keep coming up with family, friends, or lovers, you're seeing the rub in the inner dialogue between you and you—where your inner dialogue is stuck. You won't be able to change those patterns until you recognize where the strife is internally.

Start slowly and compassionately.

Dialogue is by far the hardest part of B.F.D., so don't be too hard on yourself if you're struggling with engaging positive self-talk and changing your personal statement to a power statement. They take time and practice.

With enough practice, you'll start to hear a difference in your inner dialogue. The changes will be subtle at first. The next time something goes wrong, or you experience a disappointment, you might hear your personal statement, but it might be quieter, and your power statement may come in to override it. You might start a dialogue about yourself that isn't very kind, and you may find yourself pausing and saying, "No, that's not how my compassionate friend would speak to me," and you'll change your tune mid-sentence.

These are small steps on the way to big gains. Remember, our thoughts are always creating our reality. Therefore, it stands to reason that if you are changing your thoughts, even in small ways, you are slowly changing your reality. And before you know it, your reality will be a lot closer to 10 on the Dime scale, all because you are talking to yourself, about yourself, in an accommodating, compassionate, and kind way—the way you deserve to be talked to.

CHAPTER FIVE

Broadcasting

WHAT IS THE energy that you're broadcasting to the world around you?

By now you've practiced your B.F.D., but you might have lost sight of why you're practicing it. That's okay. There's a lot to take in, and it's easy to lose sight of why you're making these subtle but very important changes to your daily habits.

So, why did I spend all this time bending your ear about B.F.D.?

In short, your energy determines your mood. You're not managing emotions, which is a much more difficult and often futile task; you're managing your energy, which will

ultimately determine your mood. B.F.D. is energy management to manage your mood.

. . . .

Energy is everything!

. . . .

When you have energy, in the way you interact with the
world and the extra capacity you bring to your daily existence, you're in a better mood and mental state. That feeling
is then going to determine your experience of life.

You want to manage this energy because your channel
matters. Not to overstate the case or be melodramatic, but
your energy is *everything*. What you give out you get back.
In other words, whatever channel of energy you're on is
what's going to return to you. I am sure you've experienced
this at some level.

When you're on a high channel, you seem to run into
opportunity, or maybe you think about someone and they
call you. From a high channel, you have more access to
creative solutions and are able to connect with people more
easily. You're able to anticipate the moment more easily.
High channel energy manifests itself in so many beneficial
ways.

I talk a lot about this with the leaders I coach. When
they're on a high channel, they're able to avoid conflict by
having the energy to look up and observe and anticipate.
They're proactive instead of being in survival mode on a low
channel, where they don't have the capacity to see what is
happening around them and, therefore, must be reactive.

If you wake up in the morning feeling like a 2 and you don't learn to manage that, look out, because it's not going to be a good day. That's not predestined or predetermined. You can change the outcome by managing your energy before you face the world.

My morning routine used to take about two hours, and I really tried not to see anyone until I'd completed it because I knew I needed to get myself to a 10 to have the kind of day I wanted. I understand that not everyone has the luxury of time to do that—and now that I have a toddler I never do—but that's my ideal situation. Everyone will develop their own methods and routines to climb to a Dime before facing the world. Mine have shortened through necessity, and yours will change over time too.

This is your reminder to aim for Channel 10 every day. Tune in to Radio Dime!

Better yet, learn to be the Radio Dime DJ!

What's on Your Broadcast?

Like the strange and wonderful creatures of the deep ocean, it's been shown that humans emit light, and the level of light can change with your energy and mood.

A 2009 Japanese study proved that the "human body literally glimmers." The naked eye can't detect it, but "ultraweak photon emission is known as the energy released as light through the changes in energy metabolism." [1]

The study showed that in the late afternoon, when we're burning the most energy, we glow brightest. And it's not because we're releasing body heat. It's because our molecules are getting excited and speeding up.

Take a few moments to think about that: when we have more energy, when we're excited, we *glow*, and as I mentioned earlier, people around us can sense our vibrations and subconsciously mirror them. So, I want you to consider what energy you're broadcasting to the world around you. The invisible radio waves that you emit all day, every day.

You have the ability to control the level of light you emit with your energy, and the energy you put into the world comes from the frequency you're broadcasting on.

Many people believe they're already on a high frequency, especially those in positions of power. The number one question/comment I get after my seminars is "Jill, I am on a high channel, but the people around me (my colleagues/ spouse/family) are on a low channel!"

They always have so much conviction that it's not them! That's a red flag to me, because putting the low channel blame on others also comes from a lower channel! They are saying that they would feel better but other people are "making" them feel worse.

The fact is, no one can bring you down without your consent.

We often want connections so badly that we'll adjust to other people's channels to manufacture a connection. If you are on a high level and your companion is on a lower channel, it can seem like care and compassion—a sort of empathy, even—to meet them at their level, but it can also be enabling.

In this situation, if a 10 is meeting up with a 2 for a morning coffee, the 10 should act as a 10. That 10 should hit the 2 with a sunny smile and a boisterous "Good morning!" But more often than not, what ends up happening is that the 10 will lower themselves under the guise of empathy and give the 2 a sympathetic head tilt and a soft "How are you today?" Our tendency is to go right to matching people. That instinct diminishes all the work the 10 has done for themselves, and it allows the 2 to stay at a 2.

Trying to match someone else's energy makes people tired. I work with a lot of personal trainers, and one thing I've noticed is that they're exhausted at the end of the day. It's not all the working out—these are the fittest people around, and the fitness aspect energizes them. No. It's their poorly managed energy as they constantly try to match their clients, most of whom are struggling with their own energy, that is exhausting them. One minute they're a 2, then an hour later they're a 6, then they meet a 4 and have to re-adjust again. That is not energy management. It's also not living authentically, which is another drain on your energy.

The opposite is also true. If a 6 is hanging out with a 10 and trying to match that 10, they are going to be exhausted. They aren't there yet, and that's okay. Better to let the good vibes from the 10 be aspirational and empowering. Bask in the glow and determine what you can do to get to that level at your own pace.

Another trend I've recognized in clients is that they may feel great, they're heading up that ladder to a Dime, but they tell me their spouse or partner is a 5. They love the other person so much that they end up focused on what channel they're on. It's a form of love.

The tendency, especially in an intimate relationship like a marriage, is to give your attention to someone else's chan-nel so frequently that no one's helping anyone and both people are stuck at 5. And unlike pocket change, two nickels don't equal a Dime.

If one person is living like a Dime, however, they might see the lower energy but not feel the need to lower their own. The kind and loving thing, in fact, is not to. Broadcasting higher-level energy can empower and embolden someone, especially a person so closely connected and in your broadcast range.

When you're faced with someone who is on a much lower channel, you need to be aware of their energy level and use your B.F.D. protective shield. Resist the urge to bring yourself down to their level. Instead, rise above it and bring them up with you.

Notice what you do with your body around certain people or in certain situations. Sit up, be attentive, and use a calm but strong voice. Focus on how amazing the person is and use your dialogue—speak kindly about them, both in your head and out loud. These things will help to maintain your channel, which is hugely important because you worked hard to get it. But—and here is where it comes full circle—by being yourself, you are being kind and loving, and that is the type of thing that will help lift a person up their own Dime scale. Good vibes are contagious. Be the contagion!

Ask for the Full Can—You Deserve It

When I first started my business, I would get very excited about traveling for work. It felt like a big deal to be on a flight I didn't pay for, on my way to share my own creation. I'd put on my white Under Armour athleisure suit (yes, it was as spectacular and functional as you're imagining), settle into my seat, fire up my iPad with episodes of *Modern Family* ready to go, and reflect on how I was Diming.

I always like to have the entire can of club soda when I'm flying. Not a little plastic glass of it, but the whole thing. Riding that wave of confident Diming in the early days, I would ask the flight attendant for the can of club soda when they came by to offer drinks, but I would often get a bit of attitude back. Granted, it can be a difficult job, but I was being polite and I wasn't being unreasonable.

"Uh, I don't know if we have enough," they'd say. Or "I have to go to the back and see." Or just a straight-up "No."

I was taken aback. I was pretty sure I was a Dime. How were they not catching on to that energy? How could I be attracting a less than 10 response when I'm a 10? Don't they like my leisure suit? Is my entire philosophy wrong?!

Either I'm not the 10 I think I am, or I'm expecting them to be on a low channel and I'm sliding down the scale to meet them.

Eventually I realized that I was expecting the flight attendant to be bothered by my request and that would affect the way I asked. With a sheepish smile I would say, "If it's not too much trouble, could I maybe have the whole can?"

I was a 5 in my ask. I was unclear, hopeful, and screwing up their nervous system with my uncertainty.

They were picking up on a confused broadcast, so they'd fumble and I'd think they were being rude. But then they'd be nice to the person behind me. It was my fault. I'd put out 5 energy and then attracted that negative part of them. What I put out came back to me.

When I asked like a 5, they would think, "It's not easy for me," or "I don't want to give every person a whole can." They also thought I was asking permission for the whole can, not asking for the whole can, which created more chaos in the flight attendant's mind.

• • • • • • • • • • • •

Clear is kind.

• • • • • • • • • • • •

Clarity is key. You don't want any static in your broadcast. Being clear is kind, being clear is certain, and certain is high channel.

I started to simply smile and say, "I'd like the whole can please. No glass, and no ice." And boom, I would get it every time, usually with a friendly conversation and pleasant human interaction.

We often ask like a 5 because we think we're being polite, but you can be a 10 and still be polite, while also easing the other person's nervous system.

When I get the full can now, I take a picture of it with the hashtag #Diming and put it on my social media stories. If you follow me and see that, you now know when I'm having a Dime moment. (And now that you know the story, your mission, should you choose to accept it, is to get the whole can and post a picture of it. Be a little mysterious and let others wonder. It'll be our little can collective, and you'll bring me a lot of joy.)

If being clear is kind, then creating uncertainty is unkind. Be clear and polite as you command with certainty.

The problem is, we get into trouble when we frame our requirements as if they are optional. (I find this happens a lot with women in business.)

"If I might be able to add something." Have you ever heard that in a meeting? Brutal. "If I might" is passive and weak. It is waiting for permission instead of commanding with certainty.

The statement you want is "I have something to add."

See how that sounds totally different? It's a completely different energy.

When you have certainty in your voice, you feel more certain yourself. Certainty is a human need that everyone's craving right now. We want to know the future is safe; we want to know what is going to happen. We look for people who are going to give us that feeling of reassurance.

Consider this in the way you engage with young people too, as they require that kind of safety and guidance. If you're a teacher and say, "Maybe you guys could sit," you think you're being polite, but the students' nervous systems are confused. They don't know what you want them to do, so they don't listen or they misbehave, and you take that personally.

You could say, "Sit down now, students" with a smile instead. Your tone doesn't have to be aggressive, but your words are clear. It's about the language that we choose and the frequency that we're on.

And speaking with certainty doesn't mean you have to know all the answers, or even be correct. If you genuinely don't know the solution to a problem or are confused by an idea, don't shy away from it. Ask for help in a clear way. People will want to help you more if you are forward and clear.

We must learn to be specific in our communication. Being direct allows people around us to understand what is expected of them, and as a result, their nervous system can relax.

Being clear is an act of kindness. Speak like you deserve it and accept that whole can from the flight attendant. Try it with me now. "Whole can, please. No glass, no ice."

You're not pulling Jedi mind tricks on flight attendants. You're being clear and kind and broadcasting on Radio Dime. Accept the club soda unapologetically.

And in case you missed the metaphor, the full can represents whatever it is you might think you don't deserve and hem and haw and worry about asking for. Or going for.

If you think you're being a bit difficult, don't be surprised if you don't get what you want. And when we don't get what we want, we start to feel victimized. You'll then start broadcasting lower energy. That's a vicious circle.

So, flip your behavior. If you want to have a fun life, start being a fun person. If you want to have exciting things come your way, manage your energy so you're ready to find and accept them. The channel you're on is all you can expect to receive.

Every day, we experience things that we perceive as positive and negative, perception being the key action. Our energy level dictates how we can receive information and how we can broadcast it back into the world.

Be confident in your desires and realize that you deserve the best that life has to offer. It's a fact that you get back what you put in, and it's time to start embracing that. Be a 10 and you'll elicit level 10 engagements from those around you.

• • •

I'm so excited you're on this journey, because one person on a higher channel is more powerful than hundreds of people on a lower channel. We need to reverse some trends in society and the direction in which a lot of the world is traveling. Your energy is the perfect place to start.

So just worry about yourself, darling. Get yourself on Channel 10 and people will come meet you there. Not everyone is willing or able—people can only meet you as far as they've met themselves—and it might not be who you expect, but they will come. Remember I said that.

Broadcast from Channel 10 and you'll be surprised by the things that come to you. Things that you can't even imagine from your present state will start to happen. It's so exciting.

Now go get yourself that can of soda and *glimmer*.

Life starts now.

Epilogue

IN THE INTRODUCTION TO THIS BOOK, I shared with you that I had a baby during the COVID-19 pandemic, all while living in a new city without a partner and trying to balance being a new single mom with running my business.

In an episode of her podcast, *We Can Do Hard Things*, called "What We Win When We Lose It All," Glennon Doyle spoke with guest Jen Hatmaker about moments in life when your proverbial house is being burned to the ground (as I and many others felt was happening in 2020). When that happens, you go through phases of shock, pain, and suffering because it's happening, but then you reach the phase of rebuilding your house. You didn't want to start fresh and rebuild, but you had no choice. Then one day you get to the part where you realize you love the new house and might even like it more than the one you started with.

This is emblematic of my story thus far. There were moments when I was angry my original plan wasn't unfolding as I'd hoped, and I raged that my house had burned down.

But I did start to rebuild, even as I faced a lot of internal resistance. And during the rebuild I realized I needed to heed my own lessons more than ever. I consciously used the tools of my energy management program on a regular basis—B.F.D. was the wallpaper inside the new structure— and continuously assessed where I was on the Dime scale. I allowed whatever emotions that arose to be welcomed, then applied my tools to shift my energy and come back to my true self. My Dime self.

How did this happen?

(Cue "Brand New Me" by Alicia Keys as you envision the following montage.)

As my house burned down, the smoke from the flames caused me to lose sight, momentarily, of the concepts I'd created to excel at life.

But when the smoke cleared a little, I had more clarity.

Body: When my daughter was about six months old and able to sit up in her stroller, I would go out running every morning at 5:30. Rain, snow, dark, locusts, whatever. We went. I thought about my posture and facial expression. I moved.

Focus: During these runs I would think about my ideal situation for the day and the week, and I'd create images of the new future I was building, even just in my mind at first, before I took any concrete steps.

Dialogue: I listened to great music. I found my power statements and repeated them, over and over. I would find times during the day to do a little daydreaming through journaling and meditating.

With the help of the best nanny in the world (I'm forever grateful for Nanny Coco. Thank you!), I was able to focus on work, knowing my daughter was having the best time. She was safe, loved, and usually laughing.

Broadcasting: I dug deep into my work and created a digital dashboard to make coaching my energy management program scalable, and I crafted a course to certify coaches to help teach my material. I piloted a middle school program for youth. I worked with some great clients and companies.

Living in my own concepts on a daily basis reminded my whole being of what I knew to be true. As time went on, I was able to speak about these principles with more clarity and passion. I was the living embodiment of the very concepts that I had created and encouraged in so many others.

. . .

Since those early days of Diming in my new life, I've taken everything that I created for corporate settings and tailored it to my first love: sports. I've had the opportunity to work with Rugby Canada and Canada Basketball, and the youth programs I started have been growing through the support of some fantastic sponsors and have impacted hundreds of young players already.

I have realized that the true love of my life is my Baby Dime, my daughter. No matter how everything happened, she was meant to come into my life and give me a new perspective and teach me about a love I didn't know existed. We were meant to be together like this for this time.

When I finally accepted I was raising her alone, I felt lighter, I felt stronger, and I had the energy to give to the things that matter most to me. First my daughter, then my precious family and friends, and then the exciting career paths that are opening up for me as I focus on them. I can provide for my daughter myself, and I now have the energy to create opportunities and accept the ones that find me. Our team of two is strong and happy.

I have chosen authenticity over negativity, and, in part because of that, I chose my energy. When I was angry and resigned that my house was burning down, I was missing important moments of my life and I was getting sick. Now I'm at peace and my energy is strong. Nothing is perfect, and there are hard days, for sure. But I'm in control. I'm choosing what I focus on. I can truly say that I'm so glad it worked out this way and I truly love the new space I've built.

This experience of digging myself out of a challenging situation has changed me on every level. I like who I am today. I like who I am in the process of becoming.

I am so grateful for the B.F.D. principles and being able to draw on them in good times and bad. I love getting to talk about them, I love being able to share them, and I hope I can shift your thinking so you can enjoy your life and experiences more and more, regardless of your conditions.

Thank you for allowing me to share my energy management program with you. Please share your triumphs with me—a full can of soda, or whatever Diming looks like for you.

#diming

#beadime

#energymanagement

@be_a_dime

jillpayne.ca

Workbook

ARE YOU EXCITED to start your Diming journey? I'm excited for you because this is the fun part! You get to put all you've learned into action and apply it to your personal situation. I have been taking CEOs, athletes, and celebrities through an extensive 12-week coaching program since 2014, and in this workbook you'll find many of the activities they participate in.

By now you understand the benefits of energy management. It isn't rocket science, although when you are in a rut, it can feel like it is that hard. But I know you've got it in you. You know you've got it in you. So, let's get after it!

This workbook is designed to kick-start your march to living a 10-out-of-10 life, or as close to it as you're able on any given day. Some days will be harder than others, but with the knowledge you've gained and the self-exploration you'll do through the activities in this workbook, you'll be able to take detailed positive steps forward, even when the going gets tough.

And on the hardest of hard days, this workbook can serve as a reminder of how far you've come and of your hopes, dreams, and goals. Never lose sight of those.

Homing In on Your Current Dime Levels

Do you feel stuck? Are you in a loop of recurring excuses? Are you happy? Stressed? Motivated? Anxious? Pumped? Slumped? On a scale of 1 to 10, how energetic do you feel?

Start by considering how you're really feeling, all the way from your toenails to your scalp. Think about every area of your life. Right now, in this moment, where are you on the scale from 1 to 10 (circle one for each category)?

RELATIONSHIPS

1   2   3   4   5   6   7   8   9   10

LOVE

1   2   3   4   5   6   7   8   9   10

WORK/CAREER

1   2   3   4   5   6   7   8   9   10

FINANCES

1   2   3   4   5   6   7   8   9   10

HEALTH

1   2   3   4   5   6   7   8   9   10

• • •

Next, take a moment to write out (using a word or short phrase) how you feel now as it correlates to the score you just gave yourself in each category listed on the previous page. Beside that word, write what you *want* to feel. (And if you ranked yourself a 10, think about what's happening in each area of your life that's making it a 10.)

	How you feel now	What you want to feel
Relationships		
Love		
Work/Career		
Finances		
Health		

• • •

Here is another exercise to get you further dialed in to your current energetic state.

How was your day? Simple question, right? You probably get asked that just about every day, but really think about it. I want you to tell me about it, in detail. From when you awoke to this moment, recount your actions, reactions, encounters, and anything else that crosses your mind. If there isn't enough space here, use your journal or a fresh sheet of paper. (If you don't have a journal, you should get one.)

Now, take a moment to reflect on what you just wrote. Was it detailed positive? Detailed negative? Somewhere in the middle? Did you talk a lot about other people or mostly about yourself? Were you kind? Were you mean? Did elements of your day make you feel happy? Joyful? Angry? Frustrated? Sad? Was your day, on balance, a good day? A bad day? A typical day?

List the different elements of your day (your actions, reactions, encounters, etc.) that stand out to you as you reflect on your writing. Please identify each using the following scale:

1	2	3	4	5	6	7	8	9	10
NEGATIVE	DETAILED	NEGATIVE	GENERALLY		NEUTRAL		POSITIVE	GENERALLY	POSITIVE	DETAILED

Action, Reaction, Encounter	Score

Overall, how do you feel your day stacked up? You can use this and the scores you gave yourself above as a general starting point for where you are at *right now* on your overall Dime score.

Are you pleasantly surprised? A little worried? Totally mystified? Wherever you are, it's okay. I promise. We all have to start somewhere.

The good news is that the exercises in this workbook are going to help you live closer to a 10-out-of-10 life. You are doing it! Self-exploration and self-examination are the first steps. You are beginning to Dime! WAY TO GO!

Body Exercises

In chapter 2 I introduced you to the idea of B.F.D., and in chapter 3 I expanded on the energy management principles that govern the body. Remember:

- **POSTURE:** When you stand tall, you tell your nervous system that you are confident and capable. You remind yourself that whatever you are doing is important.

- **SMILING:** When you smile, you remind your body that you are feeling good and that good things are happening, or are at least possible. Smiling also lets you know that there is no danger in your immediate surroundings. If a tiger was chasing you, you would not be smiling.

- **BREATHING:** Deep belly breaths send your whole nervous system the signal that the future is safe. You are safe.

- **VOICE:** Your voice reflects your energy level, and it also helps to create it.

- **MOVEMENT:** The more of your body your move, the more energy you will feel.

Actively engaging these energy management principles is proven to increase your happiness and your health, and thus provide you with more energy to tackle your day like a Dime!

Take a minute to really think about ways in which you can add elements from each of these principles to your day. For example, you could add a routine, like taking a daily walk after lunch, or you could do something sporadically, like smiling at yourself when you see your reflection. Please fill out the areas below.

POSTURE:

....

....

....

SMILING:

....

....

....

BREATHING:

....

....

....

VOICE:

....

....

....

MOVEMENT:

....

....

....

ROUTINES

Need a hack for adding more body to your day? Simply create a morning routine!

What you do in the first hour of your morning can determine the course of your whole day. Acknowledge and embrace your body. Celebrate your body with dance, deep breathing, meaningful stretching, or engaging movement as part of your morning ritual. You can personalize your routine to best suit your channel when you wake up. Use it to create energy that will propel you through your day and enable you to face any challenges head-on with a positive approach. Spend a minimum of five minutes bringing your body to life. Are you a 10? Don't leave the house until you're at least going in that direction.

Rituals create empowerment. What will you introduce into your morning routine?

MY FIVE-MINUTE MORNING ROUTINE:

....

....

....

....

....

Now that you've built a morning routine, how could you alter your evening routine? Winding down can also help you sleep, and we all know the importance of rest. I recommend that you separate yourself from your screens as part of your evening ritual and focus on your body again by consciously relaxing each part of your body as you lie in bed. Start with easing the tension in your jaw—we carry a lot of stress there—and work your way down. By the time you hit your toes you might well be in Dreamland.

MY FIVE-MINUTE EVENING ROUTINE:

....

....

....

....

....

SOMATIC MOVEMENT EXERCISES

Somatic movements are done with the intention of focusing on the internal experience of the movement rather than the external appearance or result. They are performed slowly and require internal focus and attention to learn how the body responds. It's all about the process—it's the quality of the movement, not the quantity, that matters.

*Do not try these if you're unable to stretch or move in certain ways. They shouldn't be painful. Find variations that are gentle on your body. The recommendation is to do each one for five minutes a day, but tailor that to your body and schedule as needed.

- **HANG YOUR HEAD**
Stand up straight, with your feet rooted to the floor. Slowly hang your head, letting it fall as far down as it will comfortably go. As you do, notice how the muscles in your neck are feeling. Also notice how that neck movement has affected nearby muscles, joints, and tissues, like those in your shoulders and upper back. Identify an area that feels tense and explore how that tension feels. Notice how it feels to settle into the stretch. Try to release some of the tension you feel.

- **THE ARCH AND FLATTEN**
If you experience back pain, the arch and flatten allows you to release and then regain control of the muscles in your lower back and abdominals. Lie on your back with your feet flat on the floor, hip-distance apart, and your knees bent. Take a deep breath, noticing how the muscles in your lower back and abdominals move as you breathe. Gently arch your back, bringing your belly upward and pressing

your glute muscles and feet into the floor. Stay here for as long as feels comfortable. Then, slowly lower your back and flatten it against the floor. Repeat the movement very slowly, scanning the muscles in your torso for any tension and trying to release it.

- **NECK RELEASE**

Tuck your chin into your chest, relaxing into the stretch slowly while you take deep breaths. Release your chin and tilt your head to one side and then the other to balance out your neck. Repeat.

- **SEATED CAT-COW**

Sit in a kneeling or cross-legged position. Place your hands on your knees, then inhale and pull your chest upward, stretching and opening the front side of your body, including the front of your neck (if you can). Then, exhale and curl into yourself, tucking your chin into your chest and rounding your back. Repeat.

- **SUPINE SPINAL TWIST**

Lie on your back with your legs flat, and bring your arms out to your sides with your palms facing down so your body is in a T position. Bend your right knee so it points upward, then slowly drop your right knee over to the left side of your body, twisting your spine and lower back and stacking your hips. Turn your head toward your right fingertips. Carefully release the twist so your hips fall back to the floor, then repeat with the other side.

- **WATERFALL**

Lie down on your back with your arms alongside you, palms facing up. Bring one knee at a time up to your chest, then straighten both legs up, keeping your knees slightly bent if you find that is more comfortable for you. Hold this position for a few gentle, slow breaths. When you are ready to come out of the pose, bend one leg into your chest at a time, then place your legs on the ground.

- **SEATED TORSO CIRCLES**

  Seated in a cross-legged position, with your hands resting on your knees, gently rotate your torso in clockwise circles in time with your breaths, then counterclockwise for the same number of rounds. Focus on isolating the movement and keeping your sit bones down and your legs steady.

- **BRIDGE POSE**

  Lie on your back with your knees bent and your feet flat on the floor, hip-distance apart, toes pointing forward. Place your arms alongside you with your palms facing down. Pressing down on your palms and feet, slowly raise your hips off the floor so you are making a "bridge" with your body, stopping when your hips are lined up with your knees. Try not to let your hips dip while you hold for a few breaths, then carefully release your hips back to the ground before repeating the bridge movement.

Focus Exercises

Whatever we focus on we feel, and whatever we focus on we find! We need to practice the concept of moving our minds onto the ideal situation and away from problems.

SCHEDULE AN IDEAL SITUATION

Start with this daily exercise. Be specific. Dream it up. Even if the day doesn't go the way you've outlined, you're exercising your looking-to-the-future-and-imagining-what-you-actually-want muscle.

Time	Event	Ideal Situation
6AM	Wake up	Wake up rested, on your own, with no screaming toddlers. There's time to have a coffee and meditate before the family wakes up.

(You can use this area for today, but I suggest using your own journal to write down what your ideal situation is, each and every day.)

TURNING YOUR PROBLEMS INTO IDEALS

Practicing what you focus on in a challenging time is one of the most powerful shifts you can make. For the following exercise, think of something big or small, something you have been ruminating on, and think of how it could work out in the ideal way.

1   Write down one thing you've been worried about recently.

....

....

....

2 Write what the ideal situation would be.

....

....

....

3 How will you feel if the ideal situation comes to fruition?

....

....

....

4 What can you do now to feel that emotion?

....

....

....

UNDERLYING EMOTIONS

We tend to focus on the external things we want, the things we think will give us a certain feeling. In this exercise we are going explore what the emotion behind the "thing" you want is. Goals are great, but instead of getting consumed by chasing them, take some time to realize what the desire is behind the "thing." You can still go after it, but you can learn to feel the emotion before the *thing* is here.

What are your top three "six-pack" goals? List three things you want: (example: Own my own house.)

1

. . . .

. . . .

. . . .

2

. . . .

. . . .

. . . .

3

. . . .

. . . .

. . . .

Now list the ways these goals will make you feel: (example: Safe and stable.)

1

....

....

....

2

....

....

....

3

....

....

....

How can you make yourself feel these things right now? (example: Grounding yoga. Deep breathing. Smiling.)

1

....

....

....

2

....

....

....

3

....

....

....

Through exploring your goals from above, you have discovered the feelings you want to feel. Now is the time to take the powerful step of giving yourself that feeling through your physical body.

Write down what you could do in each of the five categories below to access the feelings you decided you wanted in the previous exercise.

Use the tools available to you to get the feeling you're searching for. Here is an example for the desire to feel safety:

POSTURE: If I felt safe, I would stand strong, confident, and upright.

SMILING: If I felt safe, I would be smiling because I would know there are no dangers in my environment.

BREATHING: If I felt safe, I would breathe into my belly and access my diaphragm and my parasympathetic nervous system.

VOICE: If I felt safe, I would speak clearly with good tone and volume. I would speak my truth.

MOVEMENT: If I felt safe, I would move freely and take up space.

Now it's your turn.

POSTURE:

....

....

....

SMILING:

....

....

....

BREATHING:

....

....

....

VOICE:

....

....

....

MOVEMENT:

....

....

....

Practice it! Everything we want is based purely on the way we think it will make us feel.

GRATITUDE ATTITUDE

When we focus on the details, we feel them more, whether it is detailed negative or detailed positive. Take this opportunity to think about what you are grateful for, then get specific about the exact aspects or details of that thing for which you're grateful. Focus on the positive details.

List five things you're grateful for (think about all aspects of your life—relationships, career, health, finances, etc.).

1

....

....

....

2

....

....

....

3

....

....

....

4

....

....

....

5

....

....

....

Choose one of the things that make you feel grateful and get detailed positive about it.

List five reasons why that thing makes you feel grateful.

1

....

....

....

2

....

....

....

3

....

....

....

4

....

....

....

5

....

....

....

Dialogue Exercises

Dialogue is everything. The conversation you have with yourself about yourself determines the conversation you have with the broader world about who you are. Let's learn to be kind to ourselves.

MINDFUL SELF-COMPASSION

Remember Dr. Kristin Neff's mindful self-compassion (see pages 94–95). First ask yourself what situation makes you feel stressful or uneasy, and then take that situation through three more questions. Here is an example for you:

1 What is the situation?

You went on a date you were excited about, and it didn't go well.

2 How are you feeling about it?

Disappointment. Discouraged. Lonely.

3 How is this part of the human experience?

Many people have gone on bad dates. People in your situation would most likely feel what you feel. You are not wrong to feel how you are feeling.

4 What would your best friend say?

Your best friend might say, "Sweet friend, I hear that was not how you wanted it to go. You had a possible vision in your head that got you excited for the future. Now you feel sad that it's not happening now. That is hard. You are a wonderful person who is fun to be around, and you are surrounded by many beautiful friends and family who love you to bits. Your person is coming and you will know when you meet them. One day you will be happy you didn't settle. I am proud of you for putting yourself out there."

Now, it's your turn.

1 What is the situation?

....

....

....

2 How are you feeling about it?

....

....

....

3 How is this part of the human experience?

....

....

....

4   What would your best friend say?

....

....

....

YOUR POWER STATEMENT

We all have a primary statement that we say to ourselves on repeat and whenever something doesn't go well. It's a statement we have been repeating over and over since we were children. Primary statements often look something like this:

> "Something's wrong with me."
>
> "I'm not good/talented/rich/attractive/smart enough."
>
> "Why me?"
>
> "What am I doing wrong?"
>
> "What will other people think?"
>
> "Why do I have to do it all?"

These questions or statements create a target around you and tend to perpetuate the narrative of your life. The more you say these things, the more the experiences of the past are repeated, and these patterns can feed themselves and grow in power.

Creating positive affirmations is great, but even more effective is finding a specific power statement that counteracts the primary statement you say to yourself all day. So, let's find your personal power statement.

When you meet a challenge, what do you tell yourself? Let's say you had a work project blow up on you. You get in a fight with your spouse. You don't get a job or promotion that you want. In these moments, what do you say to yourself?

Find a situation in your life that you need to meet head-on. What's your primary statement?

SITUATION:

....

....

....

PRIMARY STATEMENT:

....

....

....

Based on what you now know about triggers, inner and outer dialogue, and the tools we have to change the narrative, how can you begin to change what you say to yourself?

....

....

....

Drawing on all you have reflected on, write out your power statement. (If you need help with coming up with one, I provide many ideas to get you started in the section on power statements in chapter 4 [see pages 109–115].)

....

....

....

Now start saying your power statement all the time—when you're driving, when you're walking, when you're starting the day or getting ready for bed (part of your routine!). Your primary statement is something you say unconsciously, so you need to work hard to replace it with your power statement.

Broadcasting

This is where we put it all together. What is the energy that you're broadcasting to the world around you?

I created the Be a Dime Energy Management program as a performance program, but over time it's evolved into a way to relieve anxiety, which is usually what's stopping us from performing at our best.

However, I urge you not to wait until your anxiety is rising or you're in the eye of an emotional storm. Check in with yourself regularly. I suggest putting an alarm in your phone that pops up three times a day and says "B.F.D." Use it to check in. What am I doing with my body? What am I choosing to focus on? How am I speaking to myself?

This is not a routine we've been taught. We don't get it in schools (although I'd love to change that). To bring it into your life and make a change and a difference, you have to make it a routine. Think about your:

- BODY: How's my posture? Am I smiling, breathing into my belly, using my voice confidently? Check how you're presenting yourself, and move your body to feel your blood pump and your endorphins rise.
- FOCUS: Am I worrying, and what's the ideal scenario? What's the feeling that I'm wanting? Find a source of positivity and apply all of your focus to what's great about it.
- DIALOGUE: What's my story? What could I say to myself right now? What do I need to hear from my best friend? Repeat what is most important and feels most powerful. Speak to yourself as a friend. Be supportive of yourself and your goals.

Checking in with yourself doesn't need to take hours, it can be 30 seconds each time—just 90 seconds a day. Who doesn't have time for that?

When we feel terrible, focusing on our problems and speaking to ourselves negatively, we can't use our bodies in a strong way. That's where our B.F.D. alarm comes in. When we aren't feeling good, we need to stop and assess the situation. Ring the alarm!

Ask yourself: What channel am I on? Am I a 3 who is sitting like a lump and focusing on my problems, or am I a 10 who is singing out loud and thinking about my day with excitement and anticipation? Think about your B.F.D.: How is my body? Where is my focus? What is my dialogue? How can I immediately change three things to move myself up the scale?

Write out a couple of items under each category that you can refer to when that alarm rings. This is a place for brainstorming. Be creative!

BODY:

....

....

....

FOCUS:

....

....

....

DIALOGUE:

....

....

....

DAILY B.F.D. JOURNAL PROMPTS

Journaling is a terrific way to force yourself to slow down and really check in with yourself. I've provided you with some prompts here, and I highly recommend that you get a journal and use it, and these prompts, often—daily if you can.

Body Prompt:

How do I want to feel today? How will I practice it?

Feeling I Want	How I Will Practice It
Example: To be connected	Call someone I love

Focus Prompt:

What can I celebrate today? What can I appreciate? (Go into detailed positive!)

What Will I Celebrate	What I Appreciate about It/ Them, etc.
Example: My recent workout	It was raining and I was tired because my child got up in the middle of the night, but I pushed through and did it anyway. I feel great and I'm proud of my accountability to myself.

Dialogue Prompt:

What do I need to hear from myself today? What powerful statement will I repeat to myself today?

What I Need to Hear from Myself Today	Power Statement I Will Repeat
Example: I belong at the stakeholders meeting	I am worthy of all I have achieved, and my contributions are valuable

Letter to Your Future Self

When you're feeling good and your energy is high, it's fun
to think about your future. Not because you can't wait to get
there—I mean, you do—but because while you're imagining
it, you get to feel the emotions. Feel those emotions now by
writing a letter to yourself from your future self.

Dear ....,
I know you've always wanted to know the future. You want
confirmation that your future self will be safe and that your
needs will be met. Let me reassure you, you can trust what's
coming.

    This is what will be happening by the end of the month . . .

....

....

....

....

....

....

    I love you, I trust you, and I am proud of you!

Love,
Your future self
xoxo

Ideal Situations

Write out your ideal situation in each area of your life right now. Let yourself get excited!

LOVE:

....

....

....

FAMILY:

....

....

....

FINANCES:

....

....

....

HEALTH:

....

....

....

CAREER:

....

....

....

Cheat Sheet

You know about the principles of energy management. You know your job is to choose your channel on the Dime scale. You know that much of your life path is your choice. You are in control.

You know that if you do what you have always done, you will get what you have always gotten, so let's determine now, while you are on a high channel after all of the introspective work you've done (congratulations, by the way!), how you are going to prioritize energy over everything!

Think back to the start of this workbook and the first two exercises you did regarding the core areas of life, how you rated yourself on the Dime scale, and what you want to be feeling about each of those elements. Start your personal energy management plan by considering each of those areas of your life and adopting a goal or mantra for each. I'll get you started, but you'll know instinctively when you find your own.

- **RELATIONSHIPS**
  I am going to focus on the things I love about my family and friends, and I will speak them out loud. Often.

- **LOVE**
  I am going to give my partner an A and assume good intent. I am going to speak nicely to myself and gently to them.

- **WORK/CAREER**
  I am going to do a B.F.D. check-in before I start my workday and again in the afternoon, when I usually feel a dip in energy. I know it is more about my energy than what is specifically happening at work. When I am on a high channel, I have the capacity to handle it all.

FINANCES

I am going to practice the feeling of security and freedom. I am going to walk as someone who feels confident about their finances. I am going to spend 10 minutes a day organizing my finances. A Dime a day keeps the bankers at bay.

HEALTH

I am going to focus on starting the day off right with my morning routine. When I am on the right channel, healthy eating and exercise will come naturally.

Now, it's your turn.

RELATIONSHIPS

....

....

....

LOVE

....

....

....

WORK/CAREER

....

....

....

FINANCES

....

....

....

HEALTH

....

....

....

Keep on Diming in the Real World

It's time to choose your channel. Seize the Dime, and when you feel it slip or forget the principles, refer to the list at right (and this workbook). You've done the hard work. You just need a reminder now and again when life gets in the way.

I'm not one to encourage desecrating books, but I give you permission to cut the following page out and tack it to your bulletin board or bathroom mirror or inside your fridge. Wherever you find yourself looking for inspiration.

Cut the facing page along the dotted line, and refer to it as needed. Consider it wallpaper for your mind!

- Energy is the magic factor that changes everything and is the secret to my success.
- When I live on a high channel, I have more energy and capacity.
- My energy determines my mood, and my mood determines my experience of life.
- I manage my energy through B.F.D.: Body, Focus, Dialogue.

  - **BODY:** I train my nervous system to feel elevated emotions through posture, smiling, breathing, voice, and movement.
  - **FOCUS:** I lean into thinking in a detailed positive space. I focus on the feeling and not the stuff.
  - **DIALOGUE:** I speak to myself with kindness and compassion, like my best friend .... would. I constantly repeat my power statement:

  ....

  ....

- Broadcasting: I broadcast the highest channel I possibly can because I get back what I give.
- The only person who can control my energy is me!

Acknowledgments

THANK YOU . . .

To my family and to my chosen family.

To my writing team, you made this process fun! To Mike, for helping me organize and eloquently express my thoughts on paper, and to my editor, Steve, for your gentle guidance and constant support.

To my clients, for allowing me to work with you and explain how I see the world. You helped me clarify my thoughts and beliefs, to the point that I could confidently write them all down. You challenge me, and your energy keeps me on a high channel daily. I've learned something from each and every one of you.

Notes

INTRODUCTION

1 Jon Clifton, "The Global Rise of Unhappiness," *Gallup Blog*, Gallup, September 15, 2022, https://news.gallup.com/opinion/gallup/401 216/global-rise-unhappiness.aspx.

CHAPTER 1: AN INTRODUCTION TO DIMING

1 Ryan O'Halloran, "The Power of Positive Thinking and Preparation: Broncos Quarterback Russell Wilson Leans on Lessons from Late Friend," *Denver Post*, September 11, 2022, https://www.denverpost .com/2022/09/11/broncos-russell-wilson-trevor-moawad-lessons/.

2 Amrisha Vaish, Tobias Grossmann, and Amanda Woodward, "Not All Emotions Are Created Equal: The Negativity Bias in Social-Emotional Development," *Psychological Bulletin* 134, no. 3 (2008): 383–403, https://doi.org/10.1037/0033-2909.134.3.383.

3 Tam Hunt, "The Hippies Were Right: It's All about Vibrations, Man!" *Observations* (blog), *Scientific American*, December 5, 2018, https:// blogs.scientificamerican.com/observations/the-hippies-were-right -its-all-about-vibrations-man/.

4 Andrea Tomljenović, "Effects of Internal and External Environment on Health and Well-being: From Cell to Society," *Collegium Antropologicum* 38, no. 1 (March 2014): 367–72, PMID: 24851644.

5 Viktor Emil Frankl, *Man's Search for Meaning: An Introduction to Logotherapy* (United Kingdom: Beacon Press, 1992), 110.

CHAPTER 2: BODY

1 Nicole Spector, "Smiling Can Trick Your Brain into Happiness — and Boost Your Health," *Better by Today*, nbcnews.com, November 28, 2017, https://www.nbcnews.com/better/health/smiling-can-trick -your-brain-happiness-boost-your-health-ncna822591.

2 Darcher Keltner, "Hands On Research: The Science of Touch," *Greater Good Magazine*, September 29, 2010, https://greatergood .berkeley.edu/article/item/hands_on_research.

3 M. W. Kraus, C. Huang, and D. Keltner, "Tactile Communication, Cooperation, and Performance: An Ethological Study of the NBA," *Emotion* 10, no. 5 (2010): 745–749, https://doi.org/10.1037/a0019382.

4   Amy Cuddy, "Your Body Language May Shape Who You Are," TED Talks, September 15, 2013, video, 20:45, https://www.ted.com/talks /amy_cuddy_your_body_language_may_shape_who_you_are /comments.

5   David Hochman, "Amy Cuddy Takes a Stand," *New York Times*, September 19, 2014, https://www.nytimes.com/2014/09/21/fashion /amy-cuddy-takes-a-stand-TED-talk.html.

6   Amy J. C. Cuddy, Caroline A. Wilmuth, and Dana R. Carney, "The Benefit of Power Posing Before a High-Stakes Social Evaluation" (working paper no. 13-027, Harvard Business School, September 2012), http://nrs.harvard.edu/urn-3:HUL.InstRepos:9547823.

7   Hochman, "Amy Cuddy Takes a Stand."

8   Sarah Stevenson, "There's Magic in Your Smile," *Cutting-Edge Leadership* (blog), *Psychology Today*, June 25, 2012, https://www .psychologytoday.com/ca/blog/cutting-edge-leadership/201206 /there-s-magic-in-your-smile.

9   Michael B. Lewis, "The Interactions Between Botulinum-Toxin-Based Facial Treatments and Embodied Emotions," *Scientific Reports* 8, 14720, Online Research @ Cardiff, University of Cardiff, October 3, 2018, https://orca.cardiff.ac.uk/id/eprint/114646/8/Lewis.%20 The%20interactions.pub.pdf.

10 Bryan Robinson, "New Study Shows Forming a Simple Smile Tricks Your Mind into a Positive Workday Mood," *Forbes*, August 13, 2020, https://www.forbes.com/sites/bryanrobinson/2020/08/13/new -study-shows-forming-a-simple-smile-tricks-your-mind-into-a -positive-workday-mood/?sh=110861872769.

11 University of Tennessee at Knoxville, "Psychologists Find Smiling Really Can Make People Happier," ScienceDaily, www.sciencedaily .com/releases/2019/04/190412094728.htm.

12 J. A. C. J. Bastiaansen, M. Thioux, and C. Keysers, "Evidence for Mirror Systems in Emotions," *Philosophical Transactions of the Royal Society: Biological Sciences* (August 27, 2009), http://doi .org/10.1098/rstb.2009.0058.

13 McKenna Princing, "This Is Why Deep Breathing Makes You Feel so Chill," *Right as Rain*, UW Medicine, September 1, 2021, https:// rightasrain.uwmedicine.org/mind/stress/why-deep-breathing -makes-you-feel-so-chill.

14 Holly MacCormick, "How Stress Affects Your Brain and How to Reverse It," *Scope* (blog), Stanford Medicine, October 7, 2020, https://scopeblog.stanford.edu/2020/10/07/how-stress-affects -your-brain-and-how-to-reverse-it/.

15 Jose L. Herrero et al., "Breathing Above the Brainstem: Volitional Control and Attentional Modulation in Humans," *Journal of Neurophysiology* 119, no. 1 (January 2018): 145-159, https://doi.org/10.1152/jn.00551.2017

16 Princing, "This Is Why."

17 "Diaphragmatic Breathing," *Integrative Digestive Health & Wellness: Relaxation Therapies*, UCLA Health, https://www.uclahealth.org/medical-services/gastro/wellness/wellness-approaches/relaxation-therapies#:~:text=Diaphragmatic%20breathing,rest%20and%20digest)%20nervous%20system.

18 MacCormick, "How Stress Affects Your Brain."

19 Leah Eichler, "A Confident Tone of Voice Can Speak Volumes in Itself," *Globe and Mail*, August 7, 2015, https://www.theglobeandmail.com/report-on-business/careers/career-advice/life-at-work/vocal-fry-is-not-a-feminist-issue/article25880800.

20 Eichler, "A Confident Tone."

21 Dan Bullock and Raúl Sánchez, "Don't Underestimate the Power of Your Voice," *Harvard Business Review*, April 13, 2022, https://hbr.org/2022/04/dont-underestimate-the-power-of-your-voice.

22 Bullock and Sánchez, "Don't Underestimate the Power."

23 Mayo Clinic Staff, "Exercise: 7 Benefits of Regular Physical Activity," *Healthy Lifestyle: Fitness*, mayoclinic.org, October 8, 2021, https://www.mayoclinic.org/healthy-lifestyle/fitness/in-depth/exercise/art-20048389.

24 *The Definition of "Somatic," The History of Somatic Education, and Principles of Clinical Somatic Education* (Somatic Movement Center, 2019), https://somaticmovementcenter.com.wp-ontent/uploads/2018/08/Somatic-Theory.pdf

25 Rachelle P. Tsachor and Tal Shafir, "A Somatic Movement Approach to Fostering Emotional Resiliency through Laban Movement Analysis," *Frontiers in Human Neuroscience* 11 (September 7, 2017): 410, https://www.frontiersin.org/articles/10.3389/fnhum.2017.00410/full.

26 Teresa Paolucci et al., "Improved Interoceptive Awareness in Chronic Low Back Pain: A Comparison of Back School versus Feldenkrais Method," *Disability and Rehabilitation* 39, no. 10 (May 2017): 994-1001.

CHAPTER 3: FOCUS

1 Mary West, "What Is the Fight, Flight or Freeze Response?" Medical News Today, July 28, 2021, https://www.medicalnewstoday.com/articles/fight-flight-or-freeze-response#freeze.

2 Borut Poljšak and Irina Milisav, "Clinical Implications of Cellular Stress Responses," *Bosnian Journal of Basic Medical Sciences* 12, no. 2 (May 2012): 122-126, https//doi.org/10.17305/bjbms.2012.2510.

3 Javier Horcajo et al., "The Effects of Overt Head Movements on Physical Performance After Positive Versus Negative Self-Talk," *Journal of Sport and Exercise Psychology* 41, no. 1 (February 1, 2019): 36-45, https://doi.org/10.1123/jsep.2018-0208.

4 Micah Abraham, "How to Control Muscle Weakness Associated with Anxiety," CalmClinic, March 1, 2021, https://www.calmclinic.com/anxiety/symptoms/muscle-weakness.

CHAPTER 4: DIALOGUE

1 Jack Nasher, "To Seem More Competent, Be More Confident," *Harvard Business Review*, March 11, 2019, https://hbr.org/2019/03/to-seem-more-competent-be-more-confident.

2 J. Hao and X. Du, "Preschoolers' Helping Motivations: Altruistic, Egoistic or Diverse?" *Frontiers in Psychology* 12 (April 13, 2021), https://doi.org/10.3389/fpsyg.2021.614868.

3 Davis Tchiki, "Shame: Definition, Causes, and Tips," Berkeley Well-Being Institute, https://www.berkeleywellbeing.com/shame.html.

4 Juliana Breines, "3 Ways Your Beliefs Can Shape Your Reality," *Health* (blog), *Psychology Today*, August 30, 2015, https://www.psychologytoday.com/ca/blog/in-love-and-war/201508/3-ways-your-beliefs-can-shape-your-reality.

5 Breines, "3 Ways."

6 S. G. Turner and K. Hooker, "Are Thoughts about the Future Associated with Perceptions in the Present? Optimism, Possible Selves, and Self-Perceptions of Aging," *International Journal of Aging and Human Development* 94, no. 2 (January 2021): 123-137, https://doi.org/10.1177/0091415020981883.

7 Breines, "3 Ways."

8 A. J. Crum et al., "Mind over Milkshakes: Mindsets, Not Just Nutrients, Determine Ghrelin Response," *Health Psychology* 30, no. 4 (2011): 424-429, https://doi.org/10.1037/a0023467.

9 A. J. Crum and E. J. Langer, "Mind-Set Matters: Exercise and the Placebo Effect," *Psychological Science* 18, no. 2, (2007): 165-171. https://doi.org/10.1111/j.1467-9280.2007.01867.x.

10 Hafiz, *The Gift: Poems by Hafiz, the Great Sufi Master*, trans. Daniel Ledinsky (United Kingdom: Arkana, 1999), 281.

11 Kristen D. Neff and Katie A. Dahm, "Self-Compassion: What It Is, What It Does, and How It Relates to Mindfulness," in *Mindfulness and Self-Regulation*, eds. M. Robinson, B. Meier and B. Ostafin (New York: Springer, 2015), 121–137.

12 Neff and Dahm, "Self-Compassion."

13 Catherine Moore, "How to Practice Self-Compassion: 8 Techniques and Tips," positivepsychology.com, June 2, 2019, https://positive psychology.com/how-to-practice-self-compassion/#affirmations -practice.

14 Carl G. Jung, *Memories, Dreams, Reflections*, trans. Clara Winston and Richard Winston (United Kingdom: Knopf Doubleday Publishing Group, 2011), 247.

15 Leo F. Buscaglia, *Love* (United States: Fawcett Books, 1985), 80.

16 Ethan Kross et al., "Self-Talk as a Regulatory Mechanism: How You Do It Matters." *Journal of Personality and Social Psychology* 106, no. 2 (February 2014): 304–324, http://doi.org/10.1037/a0035173.

17 Stephanie Fairyington, "Stop the 'Misery-Go-Round' of Constant Worrying," Oprah Daily, July 8, 2022, https://www.oprahdaily .com/life/health/a39638082/stop-negative-self-talk-excessive -rumination-science-backed-tips/.

18 Ethan Kross, *Chatter: The Voice in Our Head, Why It Matters, and How to Harness It* (United States: Crown, 2022), 49.

19 Bryan Robinson, "6 Ways to Harness Inner Chatter to Make—Instead of Break—Career Success," *Forbes*, February 3, 2021, https://www .forbes.com/sites/bryanrobinson/2021/02/03/6-ways-to-harness -inner-chatter-to-make-instead-of-break-career-success/?sh=1 ecdd7fa6ba6.

20 Dax Shepard, "Experts on Expert: Elizabeth Gilbert," June 6, 2019, in *Armchair Expert*, produced by Dax Shepard, Monica Padman, and Rob Holysz, podcast, https://armchairexpertpod.com/pods /elizabeth-gilbert.

21 D. K. Sherman et al., "Affirmed yet Unaware: Exploring the Role of Awareness in the Process of Self-affirmation," *Journal of Personality and Social Psychology* 97, no. 5 (November 2009): 745–764, https:// doi.org/10.1037/a0015451.

22 R. Cooke et al., "Self-affirmation Promotes Physical Activity," *Journal of Sport and Exercise Psychology* 36, no. 2 (April 2014): 217–223, https://doi.org/10.1123/jsep.2013-0041.

23 C. Logel and G. L. Cohen, "The Role of the Self in Physical Health: Testing the Effect of a Values-Affirmation Intervention on Weight Loss," *Psychological Science* 23, no. 1 (2012): 53–55, https://doi.org/10.1177/0956797611421936.

24 P. R. Harris et al., "Self-affirmation Reduces Smokers' Defensiveness to Graphic On-pack Cigarette Warning Labels," *Health Psychology* 26, no. 4 (August 2007): 437–446, https://doi.org/10.1037/0278-6133.26.4.437.

25 K. Layous et al., "Feeling Left Out, but Affirmed: Protecting Against the Negative Effects of Low Belonging in College," *Journal of Experimental Social Psychology* 69 (2017): 227–231, https://doi.org/10.1016/j.jesp.2016.09.008.

26 Catherine Moore, "Positive Daily Affirmations: Is There Science Behind It?" positivepsychology.com, March 4, 2019, https://positivepsychology.com/daily-affirmations/#science.

CHAPTER 5: BROADCASTING

1 Masaki Kobayashi, "Imaging of Ultraweak Spontaneous Photon Emission from Human Body Displaying Diurnal Rhythm," *PLOS One* (July 16, 2009), https://doi.org/10.1371/journal.pone.0006256.

Index

ABOUT THE AUTHOR

AS A MULTISPORT athlete, Jill Payne represented Canada in both sprint canoe and rugby before turning her focus to helping others, including working as a sought-after celebrity trainer. Her background in kinesiology and education eventually led Jill to her Master's in Employee Engagement & Workplace Performance. She founded Be a Dime Energy Management and began working with companies across North America—including NBC, Google, Sony, McDonald's, Pepsico, Panasonic, Boeing, JPL, and Western Union—to reinvigorate productivity, enhance corporate culture, and influence positive business outcomes. Her work has been featured in *Vogue*, *Glamour*, *Elle*, and *SELF*. Recently, Jill returned to the sports world, where she has provided mental skills and culture coaching for both national and professional teams. She lives on Vancouver Island with her daughter.

NOTES

....

....

....

....

....

....

....

....

....

....

....

....

....

NOTES

....

....

....

....

....

....

....

....

....

....

....

....

....

....

....

NOTES

NOTES

#Diming

WELCOME TO DIMING! What a ride. You've really earned it. And it doesn't have to end here.

Even the best of us may, after a time, lose sight of our path and revert to old behaviors that aren't serving us or our future plans. And I don't want that for you.

That's why I'm offering you a free one-month trial of the 12-week, three-stage program that I offer when coaching my clients. Simply scan the QR code to access Stage One: Creating Fertile Soil. It will reinforce the concepts of this book through weekly content videos, daily audio tips, and a digital version of the coaching workbook and journal. Guaranteed fun!

And for those who opt to stay on, it will prep you for Stage Two: Planting the Seed. Here we get detailed positive about what you want, where are you going, and what the future self you are creating looks like. Stage Three: Trust is all about learning to trust that if we've planted a good garden, the flowers will come. Here we learn to prepare to receive what we asked for.

A 10-out-of-10 life is already within you. Let's find it!